GCSE
Combined Science

Stephanie Anstey
Emma Dougan
Ayd Instone

HODDER
EDUCATION
AN HACHETTE UK COMPANY

The Publishers would like to thank the following for permission to reproduce copyright material.

Photo credits

Page 22: © DR KEITH WHEELER / SCIENCE PHOTO LIBRARY; Page 25: © BIOPHOTO ASSOCIATES / SCIENCE PHOTO LIBRARY

Hachette UK's policy is to use papers that are natural, renewable and recyclable products and made from wood grown in well-managed forests and other controlled sources. The logging and manufacturing processes are expected to conform to the environmental regulations of the country of origin.

Orders: please contact Bookpoint Ltd, 130 Park Drive, Milton Park, Abingdon, Oxon OX14 4SE. Telephone: +44 (0)1235 827827. Fax: +44 (0)1235 400401. Email education@bookpoint.co.uk Lines are open from 9 a.m. to 5 p.m., Monday to Saturday, with a 24-hour message answering service. You can also order through our website: www.hoddereducation.co.uk

ISBN: 978 1 5104 8107 7

© Stephanie Anstey, Emma Dougan, Ayd Instone, Hodder Education 2020

First published in 2020 by
Hodder Education
An Hachette UK Company
Carmelite House
50 Victoria Embankment
London EC4Y 0DZ

www.hoddereducation.co.uk

Impression number 10 9 8 7 6 5 4 3 2 1

Year   2024 2023 2022 2021 2020

Cover illustration © kotoffei - stock.adobe.com
Illustrations by Integra Software Serv. Ltd.
Typeset in India by Integra Software Serv. Ltd.
Printed in India

A catalogue record for this title is available from the British Library.

Contents

How to use this book

Exam Insights for GCSE Combined Science is perfect for last-minute revision and practice. This book covers 7 of the trickiest topics where students have dropped marks in recent UK exams. It focuses on the most common misconceptions and the skills that are most difficult to answer. Namely, writing extended responses, using mathematics and demonstrating practical skills.

Throughout the book, you will see different exercises alongside more traditional exam-style questions. These include:

- Worked examples – expert walkthroughs on how best to approach a question and answer it correctly.

- Be the examiner – read through and mark student answers to understand where they went wrong and the common mistakes you should avoid in your own work.

- Improve the answer – demonstrate your knowledge to re-write a student answer and pick up maximum marks.

You will also see the following features:

Knowledge recap

✳ A brief summary of the key knowledge you'll need for each topic.

Insight
Lessons that you can learn from past exams and student answers.

UpGrade
Top tips on how to pick up extra marks and improve your grade.

Fully worked solutions with mark schemes are provided in the book so you can check your answers.

About the authors

Stephanie Anstey graduated with honours from Warwick University with a bachelor's degree in biochemistry and a postgraduate certificate in education. She has taught in secondary schools in the United Kingdom and United Arab Emirates with teaching experience in A-level and IB courses. She is currently the head of KS3 science in the West Midlands. Stephanie has also worked with educational charities in South Africa to deliver science lessons and to write and deliver teacher development sessions. In addition, she is passionate about engaging learners with the science to help make the content applicable and relevant to the world around them.

Emma Dougan is a Biology lecturer and she works for an examining body as a Principal Examiner for A Level Life and Heath Science and GCSE Biology. In addition to this text, she has co-written a number of Biology and Science textbooks.

Ayd Instone BSc(hons) (Oxford Brookes) MSc (Oxford) is Head of Physics as well as Head of Enrichment and Extra-Curricular at Fyling Hall School in Robin Hood's Bay, North Yorkshire where he teaches Key Stage 3 Science, GCSE Physics and Chemistry and A Level Physics as well as running various science and technology focused clubs.

PERIODIC TABLE OF ELEMENTS

ATOMIC NUMBER — 26; SYMBOL — Fe; NAME — Iron; ATOMIC WEIGHT — 55.845; OXIDATION STATES — +2 +3

STATE OF MATTER
GAS LIQUID ARTIFICIAL UNKNOWN

- HYDROGEN
- ALKALI METALS
- ALKALINE-EARTH METALS
- TRANSITION METALS
- OTHER METALS
- SEMICONDUCTORS
- OTHER NONMETALS
- HALOGENS
- NOBLE GASES

	1 IA	2 IIA	3 IIIB	4 IVB	5 VB	6 VIB	7 VIIB	8 VIIIB	9 VIIIB	10 VIIIB	11 IB	12 IIB	13 IIIA	14 IVA	15 VA	16 VIA	17 VIIA	18 VIIIA
1	1 H Hydrogen 1.008 +1 -1																	2 He Helium 4.003 0
2	3 Li Lithium 6.941 +1	4 Be Beryllium 9.0122 +2											5 B Boron 10.811 +3	6 C Carbon 12.011 -4 +2 +4	7 N Nitrogen 14.007 -3 -2 -1 +1 +2 +3 +4	8 O Oxygen 15.999 -2	9 F Fluorine 18.998 -1	10 Ne Neon 20.179 0
3	11 Na Sodium 22.99 +1	12 Mg Magnesium 24.305 +2											13 Al Aluminium 26.982 +3	14 Si Silicon 28.086 -4 +2 +4	15 P Phosphorus 30.974 -3 +3 +5	16 S Sulfur 32.065 -2 +4 +6	17 Cl Chlorine 35.453 -1 +1 +3 +5 +7	18 Ar Argon 39.948 0
4	19 K Potassium 39.098 +1	20 Ca Calcium 40.078 +2	21 Sc Scandium 44.956 +3	22 Ti Titanium 47.867 +2 +3 +4	23 V Vanadium 50.942 +2 +3 +4 +5	24 Cr Chromium 51.996 +2 +3 +6	25 Mn Manganese 54.938 +2 +3 +4 +7	26 Fe Iron 55.845 +2 +3	27 Co Cobalt 58.933 +2 +3	28 Ni Nicke 58.693 +2 +3	29 Cu Copper 63.546 +1 +2	30 Zn Zinc 65.39 +2	31 Ga Gallium 69.723 +3	32 Ge Germanium 72.64 -4 +2 +4	33 As Arsenic 74.922 -3 +3 +5	34 Se Selenium 78.96 -2 +2 +6	35 Br Bromine 79.904 -1 +1 +5	36 Kr Krypton 83.8 0 +2
5	37 Rb Rubidium 85.468 +1	38 Sr Strontium 87.62 +2	39 Y Yttrium 88.906 +3	40 Zr Zirconium 91.224 +4	41 Nb Niobium 92.906 +3 +5	42 Mo Molybdenum 95.94 +3 +6	43 Tc Technetium (98) +4 +6 +7	44 Ru Ruthenium 101.07 +3	45 Rh Rhodium 102.91 +3	46 Pd Palladium 106.42 +2 +4	47 Ag Silver 107.87 +1	48 Cd Cadmium 112.41 +2	49 In Indium 114.82 +3	50 Sn Tin 118.71 +2 +4	51 Sb Antimony 121.76 -3 +3 +5	52 Te Tellurium 127.6 -2 +4 +6	53 I Iodine 126.9 -1 +1 +5 +7	54 Xe Xenon 131.29 0 +2 +4 +6
6	55 Cs Caesium 132.91 +1	56 Ba Barium 137.33 +2		72 Hf Hafnium 178.49 +4	73 Ta Tantalum 180.95 +5	74 W Tungsten 183.84 +6	75 Re Rhenium 186.21 +4 +6 +7	76 Os Osmium 190.23 +3 +4	77 Ir Iridium 192.22 +3 +4	78 Pt Platinum 195.08 +2 +4	79 Au Gold 196.97 +1 +3	80 Hg Mercury 200.59 +1 +2	81 Tl Thallium 204.38 +1 +3	82 Pb Lead 207.2 +2 +4	83 Bi Bismuth 208.98 +3 +5	84 Po Polonium (209) +2 +4	85 At Astatine (210)	86 Rn Radon (222) 0
7	87 Fr Francium (223) +1	88 Ra Radium (226) +2		104 Rf Rutherfordium (261) +4	105 Db Dubnium (262) +5	106 Sg Seaborgium (266) +6	107 Bh Bohrium (264) +4 +6 +7	108 Hs Hassium (277) +3 +4	109 Mt Meitnerium (268) +3 +4	110 Ds Darmstadtium (281) +2 +4	111 Rg Roentgenium (272) +1 +3	112 Uub Ununbium (285) +1 +2	113 Ununtrium (284) +1 +3	114 Uuq Ununquadium (289) +2 +4	115 Ununpentium (288) +3 +5	116 Uuh Ununhexium (291) +2 +4	117 Uus Ununseptium	118 Uuo Ununoctium (294) 0

LANTHANIDES	57 La Lanthanium 138.91 +3	58 Ce Cerium 140.12 +3 +4	59 Pr Praseodymium 140.91 +3	60 Nd Neodymium 144.24 +3	61 Pm Promethium (145) +3	62 Sm Samarium 150.36 +2 +3	63 Eu Europium 151.96 +2 +3	64 Gd Gadolinium 157.25 +3	65 Tb Terbium 158.93 +3	66 Dy Dysprosium 162.5 +3	67 Ho Holmium 164.93 +3	68 Er Erbium 167.26 +3	69 Tm Thulium 168.93 +3	70 Yb Ytterbium 173.04 +2 +3	71 Lu Lutetium 174.97 +3
ACTINIDES	89 Ac Actinium 227 +3	90 Th Thorium 232.04 +4	91 Pa Protactinium 231.04 +4 +5	92 U Uranium 238.03 +3 +4 +5 +6	93 Np Neptunium (237) +3 +4 +5 +6	94 Pu Plutonium (244) +3 +4 +5 +6	95 Am Americium (243) +3 +4 +5 +6	96 Cm Curium (247) +3	97 Bk Berkelium (247) +3 +4	98 Cf Californium (251) +3	99 Es Einsteinium (252)	100 Fm Fermium (257)	101 Md Mendelevium (258)	102 No Nobelium (259)	103 Lr Lawrencium (262)

Overview

Knowledge recap

* *Pathogens* cause infectious disease in animals and plants. Pathogens include bacteria, fungi, protists and viruses.

* *Bacteria* produce toxins which damage tissues. *Viruses* reproduce inside cells, causing damage.

* Malaria is caused by a *protist*. It is transmitted by bites from infected female mosquitos.

* Humans have a number of non-specific defence systems against pathogens including *physical barriers* and *chemical defence systems*.

* *Antigens* on a pathogen trigger a specific immune response, causing the production of specific *antibodies* and specific *memory lymphocytes*, resulting in a faster secondary response if the same pathogen returns.

* *Vaccination* introduces dead or inactive forms of a pathogen to stimulate the immune response and produce memory lymphocytes.

* *Antibiotics* are used to treat bacterial infections. Their overuse has led to some bacteria developing resistance to antibiotics.

* *Preclinical trials* of new medicines are carried out on cells, tissues and live animals. *Clinical trials* are carried out on volunteers and patients.

* *Monoclonal antibodies* are specific to one antigen so can be used to target a specific chemical or type of cell in the body.

* There are a number of different symptoms of plant disease including stunted growth, spots on leaves and discolouration of leaves (chlorosis).

* Plants have a number of physical defences (such as cellulose cell walls) and chemical defences (such as antibacterial chemicals).

* Coronary heart disease is an example of a *non-communicable disease* caused by the build-up of fat in the coronary arteries.

* *Cancer* is caused by changes in cells which leads to uncontrolled growth and division. Tumours can either be benign (harmless) or malignant (cancerous).

Practice questions

1   Explain why heart disease is not categorised as an infectious disease.   (1)

_____

2   Explain the differences between how bacteria and viruses cause disease.   (2)

_____

_____

_____

3   Explain why antibiotics cannot be used to treat malaria.   (2)

_____

_____

_____

4 Explain the difference between clinical trials and preclinical trials. (2)

_____

_____

5 Describe the difference between malignant tumours and benign tumours. (2)

_____

_____

6 Both plants and animals use physical barriers to prevent infection by pathogens. Compare the physical barriers used by plants and animals. (2)

> **Insight**
> In past exams, students have struggled to explain physical barriers to infection, instead focusing answers on the immune system. Make sure you answer the question.

_____

_____

_____

7 Some people may develop minor symptoms after being vaccinated against a disease. Suggest why this occurs. (1)

_____

8 Monoclonal antibodies can be used to deliver drugs to cancer cells in the body. This is a much more targeted treatment than using standard chemotherapy treatments. Explain why. (4)

_____

_____

_____

9 People who contract chickenpox in childhood do not normally contract it again in adulthood. Use your knowledge of the immune response to explain this. (3)

_____

_____

_____

10 A student wrote the following about a plant disease: 'When a plant contracts tobacco mosaic virus, the disease enters the phloem.'

Evaluate the quality of this statement and suggest an improvement. (2)

> **Insight**
> Students often lose marks by confusing key terms such as communicable and non-communicable disease, pathogen and disease, and immunity and resistance. Ensure you are clear on the differences between these terms.

_____

_____

_____

Extended responses

Worked example

1   Explain how monoclonal antibodies can be used in medicine for detection
    and treatment. (6)

Plan your answer to this question in the space below. Start by circling the command word and then highlight or underline any useful information. When writing your plan, consider numbering your points in the order you would write them.

> **Insight**
> Examiners warn against answers which may contain lots of correct content but which do not answer the question. If information is not relevant to the question, it will not gain any marks.

Here is a sample answer with expert commentary:

The student does receive credit for stating what monoclonal antibodies are and for giving pregnancy tests as one example of their use.

Monoclonal antibodies are specific to one binding site so can target specific cells and chemicals. This makes them ideal for detection or treatment, for example they are used in pregnancy test kits. Monoclonal antibodies are produced using mouse lymphocytes to make a specific antibody. The lymphocytes are combined with tumour cells. This produces a hybridoma. This hybridoma can divide and produce the specific antibody. The hybridoma cells are cloned to make lots of identical cells this allows a large amount of the antibody to be collected.

Most of this answer is concerned with how monoclonal antibodies are produced, in other words, the process of producing the hybridoma. While this information is correct, it does not address how monoclonal antibodies can be used, so therefore does not answer the question.

This answer would get 2/6 despite containing lots of factually correct information about monoclonal antibodies. The issue is that the student has failed to answer the question fully, writing about how monoclonal antibodies are produced rather than their uses.

Be the examiner

2 Four new chemicals have been developed which are believed to have antibiotic properties. Design an experiment using discs soaked in the chemicals to determine whether they have antibiotic properties and, if they do, which is the most effective as an antibiotic. Give details of control variables in your answer.

(6)

Read through the sample answer below and comment on what is good and bad about it.

> Take four agar plates which have bacteria growing on them. Place a disc soaked with a different chemical on each agar plate. Incubate the plates for 24 hours at 10 °C. Take the plates out and observe them. Measure the areas around each disc where no antibiotics are growing (clear areas). Any chemical with a clear area has acted as an antibiotic. The most effective antibiotic will be the chemical which has produced the largest clear area.

Use the mark scheme below to help identify how the student did. Use your comments and what you have checked off to give the answer a mark.

Level descriptors	Marks	
Indicative content • Soak discs in each of the chemicals. • Place each disc on a different agar plate which has bacteria growing on it. • Incubate the plates for 24 hours at 25 °C (these are control variables). • After incubation, any plate containing a disc soaked in a chemical with antibiotic properties would be found to have a clear area around the disc (an area with no bacteria growing). • Calculate the area of the clear area around the disc. • The disc with the largest clear area contained the most effective antibiotic. • 1 × example of another control variable: concentration of chemical on disc, diameter of discs, species of bacteria used.		☐ ☐ ☐ ☐ ☐ ☐ ☐
Level 3: Answer is detailed, clear, logically written and identifies relevant points. There is a clear description of the practical steps which would produce valid results, including calculation of the clear area around the disc and a statement that the disc with the largest clear area contained the most effective antibiotic. Suitable control variables are also stated.	5–6	☐
Level 2: Relevant points given with some logical links made although the answer is not fully clear. There is a reasonably clear description of the practical steps required but there are significant omissions. Descriptions of control variables are limited.	3–4	☐
Level 1: Relevant points given with no logical links made. Only very limited practical steps are given, with little detail and lacking in a logical order. Control variables are either not stated or are incorrect.	1–2	☐

I would give this _____/6 because _____

_____

_____

Practice question

3   Describe how vaccines can be used to prevent illness in an individual and evaluate
     their use in preventing the spread of disease in a population.   (6)

Read through the sample student answer below and make notes on how you would improve it.

> When people are vaccinated they are given a weakened form of a disease.
> This causes their immune system to respond so they are protected from
> the disease. Vaccines have been very effective at preventing the spread of
> disease although some people are against them.

Write an improved response to this question that would get full marks.

_____

_____

_____

_____

_____

_____

_____

_____

_____

Practical Biology

This is a large topic with a number of areas where practical questions could be asked. Questions in this section often focus on trials of treatment and analysis of non-communicable disease statistics.

Practice questions

1   A medical trial into a new drug to lower blood cholesterol was carried out. Some participants were given a pill containing the drug (Pill A) and some were given a pill which had no metabolic effect. Each patient who received the drug was given the same concentration. The patient's blood cholesterol was measured at the end of the trial.

Total cholesterol levels less than 200 mg/dL are considered healthy for adults, 200 to 239 mg/dL is considered borderline and above 240 mg/dL is considered a health risk. Throughout the trial the patients did not know which pill they were receiving, though the doctors did. The results from the patients given Pill A are shown in the table below.

Patient	Total blood cholesterol levels / mg/dL	
	Before trial started	After a period of treatment with Pill A
1	260	255
2	245	240
3	270	265
4	290	260

1–1 Use the above table to suggest one requirement for selecting patients for this study. (1)

_____

1–2 State what the pill with no metabolic effect was acting as and explain why it was used in the trial. (2)

_____

_____

1–3 Evaluate the effectiveness of the drug, using data to support your answer. (4)

_____

_____

_____

_____

1–4 Evaluate the efforts made to avoid bias in this trial. (3)

_____

_____

_____

2   An investigation was carried out to determine the population of bacteria in a sample of food taken from a restaurant.

2–1 During the investigation it was important to use aseptic techniques. Explain why.   (2)

_____

_____

2–2 Explain why each of the following aseptic techniques are carried out.   (2)

Flaming the neck of the culture bottle

_____

_____

Lifting the lid of the agar plate at an angle

_____

_____

> **Insight**
> Exam reports have highlighted that students generally know the steps of key practicals but don't understand why they are doing them. It is very important that you understand why you are carrying out each part of a method.

2–3 A counting method for bacteria determined that there were 15 600 bacteria in a sample. Give this number in standard form to two significant figures.   (2)

_____

2–4 A counting method determined that there were the following amounts of bacteria in a sample. Calculate the mean number of bacteria. Give your answer to two significant figures.   (1)

Number of bacteria			
1	2	3	Mean
15 600	12 100	20 100	

_____

2–5 Use the data in the table to evaluate the uncertainty of these results.   (3)

_____

_____

_____

2–6 The investigator wanted to use the data provided to assess the accuracy of the practical technique used. Explain why this would not be possible and suggest what further investigations could be carried out to allow this to be done.   (2)

> **UpGrade**
> Ensure you are clear on the differences between accuracy, precision and reliability as these terms are often confused.

_____

_____

_____

Mathematics

A common maths skill assessed in this topic is using the equation for the area of the clear area produced by antibiotic-soaked discs. This comes up in exams in questions relating to antibiotic practicals.

Worked example

1 The radius of the clear area produced by an antibiotic is 9 mm. Use the equation below to calculate the area of the clear area. Give your answer to one decimal place. (2)

area of clear area = πr^2 where $\pi = 3.14$

....

Step 1 *Substitute the values from the question into the equation.*

area of clear area = 3.14×9^2 (1)

Step 2 *Square the radius.*

area of clear area = 3.14×81

Step 3 *Multiply the two values together.*

area of clear area = 254.34

Step 4 *Round the answer down to one decimal place and give the correct unit. As the radius is measured in mm, the correct unit for area is mm².*

The area of the clear area is 254.3 mm² (1)

....

UpGrade

If you are given a value for π, you should use this rather than the value from your calculator. Using the value given will usually give you a simpler answer which will be easier to round.

Practice questions

2 Calculate the area of a clear area with a diameter of 1.42 cm. Use the equation

area of clear area = πr^2 where $\pi = 3.14$

to calculate the area of the clear area. Give your answer in mm² and to three significant figures. (2)

UpGrade

Make sure you read questions carefully to determine whether you need to give your answer in specific units. In this case a common mistake would be to assume that 10 mm² = 1 cm²; it doesn't. The easiest way to answer this question is to convert the diameter to mm at the start of the calculation.

_____

_____

_____

3 An investigation was carried out into the effectiveness of different antibacterial chemicals. Chemical A produced a clear area with radius 49 mm whilst chemical B produced a clear area with radius 45 mm. Calculate the percentage decrease in clear area when using the chemical B compared to chemical A. Give your answer to the nearest whole number and show all your working. (3)

_____

_____

_____

_____

2 Hormonal co-ordination in humans

Overview

Knowledge recap

* *Homeostasis* is the maintenance of a *constant internal environment* such as blood glucose concentration, body temperature and water balance.

* Homeostasis involves *negative feedback*. This occurs when the body detects a change in the factor under control and adjustments are made to return it to normal.

* The *endocrine system* is made up of glands that secrete hormones directly into the bloodstream.

* The *pituitary gland* in the brain is the '*master gland*'. It secretes hormones that target other glands including the thyroid gland, adrenal gland, ovaries and testes. It then causes these glands to release further hormones.

* *Insulin* is a hormone secreted by the pancreas that *lowers blood glucose concentration* by stimulating the uptake of glucose into cells. This increases the rate at which glucose is

used by cells in respiration and the conversion of glucose to glycogen.

* *Glucagon* is a hormone produced by the pancreas that *increases blood glucose concentration* by converting glycogen back to glucose.

* *Anti-diuretic hormone (ADH)* is produced by the pituitary gland. It travels in the bloodstream to its target organ, the kidneys.

* Water content in the blood is monitored by the *osmoregulatory centre*. If the concentration of water in the blood decreases, more ADH is produced; this increases the permeability of kidney tubules, causing more water to be reabsorbed into the blood.

* Hormones can be used to treat *infertility*. *Follicle-stimulating hormone (FSH)* and *luteinising hormone (LH)* can be injected to help a woman to become pregnant naturally.

Practice questions

1   The image below shows the positions of key glands in the endocrine system.

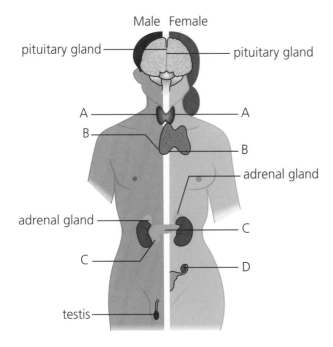

Identify each gland labelled A, B, C and D.   (4)

A _____

B _____

C _____

D _____

2 Explain why the pituitary gland is called the 'master gland'. (2)

_____

_____

_____

Insight

The word 'explain' tells you to answer in detail, with reasons. Examiner reports warn against being too vague; give an example to show what you mean.

3 Complete the below table, which gives information about some common hormones. (3)

Hormone	Produced by	Target organ	Function
ADH	Pituitary gland		Controls the concentration of water in urine
Insulin		Liver	Lowers blood glucose concentration
Oestrogen	Ovaries	Reproductive organs	

4 Describe what is meant by the term _osmoregulation_. (1)

_____

_____

5 The kidneys play a key role in osmoregulation.

5–1 Identify which hormone controls the reabsorption of water in the kidneys. Underline your answer. (1)

adrenaline   anti-diuretic hormone (ADH)

glucagon   follicle-stimulating hormone (FSH)

UpGrade

Hormones come up a lot so make sure you know the name of each hormone, where they are produced, the target organ(s) and their function(s).

5–2 Name the part of the brain where this hormone is released. (1)

_____

5–3 Describe and explain the effect of this hormone on urine production. (3)

_____

_____

_____

6 Explain how the control of water content in the blood is an example of negative feedback. (2)

_____

_____

_____

_____

7   The thyroid gland secretes the hormone thyroxine.

7–1 Give two functions of thyroid hormones in the body.   (2)

1 _____

2 _____

7–2 The below flowchart shows how the body controls the level of thyroxine in the blood. High levels of thyroxine are often treated with medication.

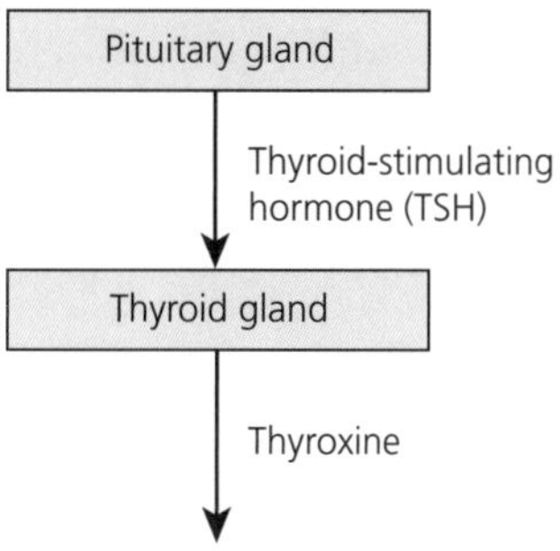

Pituitary gland

Thyroid-stimulating
hormone (TSH)

Thyroid gland

Thyroxine

Use the flowchart and your knowledge to explain how the regulation of thyroxine is an example of negative feedback control.   (3)

_____

_____

_____

_____

_____

_____

7–3 Use the above flowchart to suggest how the medication could act to restore low thyroxine levels back to normal.   (1)

UpGrade

All homeostasis involves negative feedback. You may be given an example of a negative feedback mechanism that is unfamiliar and be expected to recognise it.

_____

_____

_____

7–4 A woman who takes this medication weighs 60 kg and requires a dose of 4 mg per kilogram of body weight once a day. The medication is in a solution containing 50 mg of active ingredient in every 2.5 ml.

Calculate the dose of medication she requires each day.   (1)

_____ mg

7–5 Use your answer to 7–4 to calculate the volume of solution the woman should take each day.   (2)

_____ ml

Extended responses

Worked example

1   Describe and explain how the water content of the blood is monitored and the function of anti-diuretic hormone (ADH). (6)

Plan your answer to this question in the space below. Start by circling the command words and then highlight or underline any useful information. When writing your plan, consider numbering your points in the order you would write them.

Here is a sample answer with expert commentary:

This is good because it describes where ADH is produced. In order to access the higher marks, the answer needs to describe that the water content of the blood is monitored by the osmoregulatory centre.

ADH is produced by the pituitary gland. The water content of the blood increases when you drink too much water and less ADH is produced by the pituitary gland. When the water content of the blood decreases more ADH is produced by the pituitary gland. More water is reabsorbed by the nephrons so less urine is produced by the kidney, but it is more concentrated.

This is one of the opportunities to address the 'describe' element of the question that has not been fully taken. It should describe that less water is reabsorbed by the nephron as a result of less ADH being produced by the pituitary gland.

Good explanation linking more ADH production to more water being reabsorbed by the nephrons.

This answer would get 4/6 because the student has described ADH production. It also correctly explains how the water content of the blood is controlled by ADH when it decreases. To gain full marks, they needed to describe how the water content of the blood is monitored by the osmoregulatory centre, and explain the effect of less ADH on urine production.

2   Hormonal co-ordination in humans

Be the examiner

2 Hormones play an important role in regulating the menstrual cycle. Describe and explain how hormones affect the thickness of the uterine lining leading up to pregnancy.
(6)

Read through the sample answer below and comment on what is good and bad about it.

> The hormone FSH causes the ovaries to produce the hormone oestrogen. It causes the lining of the uterus to thicken. The high levels of oestrogen cause the release of luteinising hormone. Another hormone progesterone maintains the thick lining of the uterus if the fertilised ovum implants when pregnancy happens.

Use the mark scheme below to help identify how the student did. Use your comments and what you have checked off to give the answer a mark.

Level descriptors	Marks	
Indicative content • State that follicle-stimulating hormone (FSH) causes an ovum to mature in the ovary. • Explain that FSH stimulates the ovaries to produce oestrogen. • And that this oestrogen causes the uterine lining to thicken. • These high levels of oestrogen then switch on release of LH. • This LH then stimulates ovulation. • Progesterone will maintain a thick uterus lining if a fertilised ovum implants.		☐ ☐ ☐ ☐ ☐ ☐
Level 3: A detailed explanation of how hormones affect the thickness of the uterine lining. There is a clear linking of hormones with the correct sequence listed above. Correct terminology is used throughout.	5–6	☐
Level 2: Detailed explanations are given which clearly show how hormones affect the thickness of the uterine lining. The sequence of hormone production is written in the correct order listed. There is correct use of terms 'stimulates' and 'release'.	3–4	☐
Level 1: A short description of hormones and their role. Some linking between the hormones' different roles.	1–2	☐

I would give this _____/6 because _____

_____

_____

Practice question

3   The graph below shows the concentration of blood glucose in the body of a student after they ate a meal.

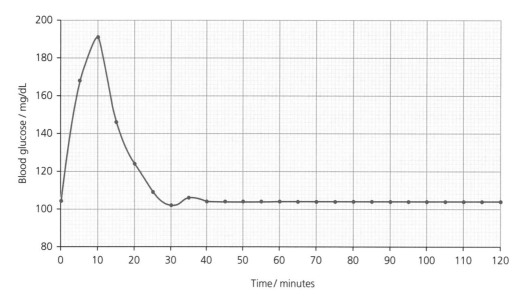

Time / minutes

Describe and explain the role of the hormones insulin and glucagon in the student's body after they had eaten the meal.   (6)

Read through the sample student answer below and make notes on how you would improve it.

> Insulin is a hormone produced by the pancreas when the concentration of blood glucose in the body is too high. Insulin lowers blood glucose levels by converting it to glycogen. Glucagon is produced when blood glucose goes down.

Write an improved response to this question that would get full marks.

_____

_____

_____

_____

_____

_____

_____

Mathematics

Examiner reports show that many students struggle with percentage calculations as well as analysing graphs and tables. In hormonal co-ordination questions, you may need to calculate percentages of blood or water in a human body or use graphs to analyse a trend.

Worked example

1   The table below shows the main inputs for water in the body.

Plot the data as a bar chart. (3)

Step 1 *Label the x-axis 'Input of water'.*

Step 2 *Label the y-axis 'Volume / cm³'.*

Step 3 *Choose an appropriate scale for the y-axis.*

Step 4 *Plot drink as 1400, food as 800 and metabolic water as 300.*

Input of water	Volume / cm³
Drink	1400
Food	800
Metabolic water	300

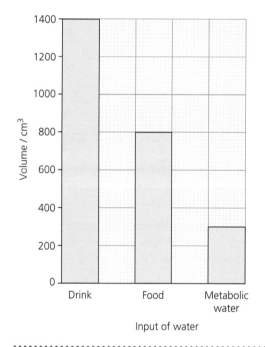

> **Insight**
> Examiner reports show that students commonly lose marks by not labelling axes fully with units and by not selecting an appropriate scale.

Be the examiner

2   The kidneys receive 1200 cm³ of blood per minute; 700 cm³ of this is blood plasma. During ultrafiltration the kidney produces 125 cm³ of filtrate per minute. Calculate the percentage of blood plasma that becomes filtrate. Give your answer to one decimal place. (2)

Looking at the three answers below, work out which one is correct and why the two others are incorrect.

A $125 \div 700 = \underline{0.18\%}$

B $125 \div 700 \times 100 = \underline{17.9\%}$

C $125 \div 1200 \times 100 = \underline{10.4\%}$

Answer _____ is correct.

Answer _____ is incorrect because _____

Answer _____ is incorrect because _____

Practice questions

3 The table below shows the water lost by a student who has played a game of football on a warm summer day.

Water lost by the body	Volume / cm³
Urine	2250
Sweat	600
Breath from lungs	450
Faeces	100

3–1 Plot the data as a bar chart on the axes given. (3)

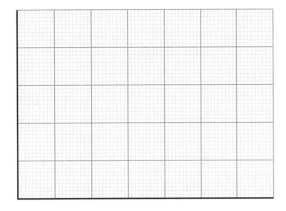

3–2 Calculate the percentage of water lost by the student as sweat. Give your answer to two significant figures. (3)

_____

_____

_____

4 Diabetes is a condition in which sufferers cannot properly regulate blood glucose levels. The table below shows the number of people in two countries with diabetes from 2012 to 2016.

	Number of people with diabetes	
Year	Country A	Country B
2012	75 837	167 537
2013	79 072	173 299
2014	81 867	177 212
2015	84 836	183 348
2016	88 305	188 644

Use data from the table to describe the trend in the number of people with diabetes from 2012 to 2016 in country B. (2)

_____

_____

_____

3 Plant structures and hormones

Overview

Knowledge recap

* Plant tissues include epidermal tissue, palisade mesophyll, spongy mesophyll, meristem, xylem and phloem. Plant organs include the root, shoot and leaf.

* A root hair cell has a small thin extension; this *increases the surface area* for absorption.

* Roots absorb water by *osmosis* and minerals by *active transport* from the soil.

* Meristems are regions of plant tissue in which *stem cells* are produced. Meristems are found at the very tip of the root and shoot.

* Xylem tissue is adapted for its function of *transport* as the cells have joined together into long tubes. *Lignin* in the walls provides support and strength.

* Phloem tissue is adapted for its function of *translocation* as the cells have fewer organelles which allows the sugar (sucrose) to move more

easily. The cells also have specialised end walls called *sieve plates*.

* Plant growth of stems towards light is called *positive phototropism*. More light means more photosynthesis with more glucose produced.

* *Positive gravitropism* (geotropism) is the ability of plant roots to grow downwards, which is often towards water.

* The plant hormone *auxin* causes *cell elongation*. Auxin is produced in the shoot tip and diffuses down. More auxin will move to the shaded side of the plant causing cell elongation on this side. This will cause the stem to curve towards the light.

* *Gibberellins* are other plant hormones that help with stem elongation and are involved in seed dormancy and germination. Gibberellins also help form flowers and fruits.

* The plant hormone *ethene* ripens fruit.

Practice questions

1   Name the tissue in a plant where stem cells are produced.   (1)

_____

2   Identify the process by which plants absorb minerals from the soil. Tick *one* box.   (1)

☐ diffusion

☐ active transport

☐ osmosis

☐ evaporation

3   Explain how root hair cells are adapted for their function.   (3)

_____

_____

_____

_____

_____

4 Root hair cells contain large numbers of mitochondria. Describe and explain how mitochondria are adapted for their function. (2)

____

____

____

5 Root hair cells do not contain chloroplasts. Suggest why. (2)

____

____

____

____

Insight

Examiner reports show that students often confuse mitochondria with chloroplasts. For example root hair cells contain mitochondria and *not* chloroplasts.

6 Identify the cells that control stomata. Tick *one* box. (1)

☐ phloem cells

☐ root hair cells

☐ xylem cells

☐ guard cells

7 Give *two* uses of gibberellins in agriculture and horticulture. (2)

1 ____

2 ____

8 Compare the structure and function of xylem and phloem tissues. (4)

____

____

____

____

____

____

UpGrade

You could make notes on the structure of xylem and phloem tissues and use these to help compare the structures.

9 Explain why the leaf is a plant organ. (2)

____

____

____

Extended responses

Worked example

1   The image below shows a cross-section of a leaf.

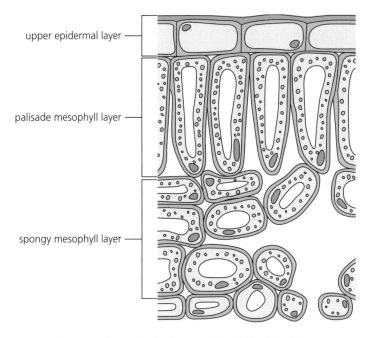

upper epidermal layer

palisade mesophyll layer

spongy mesophyll layer

Describe and explain how the labelled layers are adapted to their function.   (6)

Plan your answer to this question on a separate piece of paper. Start by circling the command words and then highlight or underline any useful information. When writing your plan, consider numbering your points in the order you would write them.

Here is a sample answer with expert commentary:

This is a vague statement, requiring more detail to gain the marks. The answer needs to describe that having lots of cells in the palisade mesophyll layer increases the surface area to absorb more light for the process of photosynthesis.

In the leaf the upper epidermis is transparent this helps it with its function. The palisade mesophyll has lots of cells to absorb light. In the spongy mesophyll gases are exchanged as the layer has a large surface area in contact with the air spaces for this.

This is good because it describes the structure of the upper epidermis. In order to access the function mark, the answer needs to explain that this allows light to pass through to the palisade mesophyll.

This describes the structure of the spongy mesophyll but does not explain how it helps it to carry out its function.

This answer would get 2/6 because the student has partially described how the structure of each layer relates to its function. To gain full marks, they need to explain in more detail how the structure *helps* the layer to carry out its function.

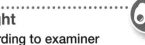

Insight
According to examiner reports, many students lose marks due to vague answers. Ensure you fully explain your answer, making links between structure and function.

Be the examiner

2   Describe and explain plant defence responses.   (6)

Read through the sample answer below and comment on what is good and bad about it.

> Plants defend themselves with physical and chemical responses. Physical defences include a waxy cuticle on the leaves which acts as a barrier and cellulose cell walls. Plants can produce chemicals to defend themselves. Some produce antibacterial chemicals to prevent bacterial infections or produce chemicals to stop them from being eaten.

Use the mark scheme below to help identify how the student did. Use your comments and what you have checked off to give the answer a mark.

Level descriptors	Marks	
Indicative content **Physical defence:** • Plants have cell walls that are thickened with cellulose to act as a barrier to resist infection by pathogens. • The waxy cuticle on leaves acts as a barrier to defend plants against infection by pathogens. • Layers of dead cells form around stems. In trees, this forms bark which falls off and so protects the plant as the pathogens fall off with it.		☐ ☐ ☐
Chemical defence: • Some plants produce antibacterial chemicals to prevent bacterial infections. • Other plants produce chemicals that are poisonous to animals that may eat them. For example, foxglove produces a chemical called digitalis.		☐ ☐
Mechanical defence: • Plants may have thorns or spines to prevent them from being eaten.		☐
Level 3: A clear description of physical, chemical and mechanical defences. At least one indicative content point from each of physical, chemical and mechanical defences with examples given. Correct terminology is used throughout with good spelling, punctuation and grammar.	5–6	☐
Level 2: Descriptions are given to include indicative content points from two types of defence mechanism with no explanations given. Satisfactory terminology is used throughout with satisfactory spelling, punctuation and grammar.	3–4	☐
Level 1: A brief description of physical, chemical or mechanical defence with no explanations given. Little use of specialised terms with errors in spelling, punctuation and grammar.	1–2	☐

I would give this _____/6 because _____

_____

_____

> **Insight**
>
> Examiner reports warn that students are unfamiliar with chemical plant defences. You could use this mark scheme to make revision notes for this topic.

Practice question

3   You have been provided with the apparatus shown below.

Design an investigation to compare the growth response of plant seedlings to light shining from above and light shining from one side. Give *two* factors that should be controlled during this investigation.   (6)

Read through the sample student answer below and make notes on how you would improve it.

> Place the seedling in the box with the hole cut on the side. Place the lamp beside the hole. After this place the other seeding in the box with the hole at the top and allow the light from the lamp to shine from above.

Write an improved response to this question that would get full marks.

Practical Biology

Practice questions

1 Describe how a light microscope could be used to produce a large, clear image of plant cells. (3)

_____

_____

_____

Insight
Examiners warn that students struggle to explain how to focus a microscope. Make sure to revise the required practicals to remind yourself of the steps involved.

2 The image below shows a section through part of a leaf as viewed by a light microscope.

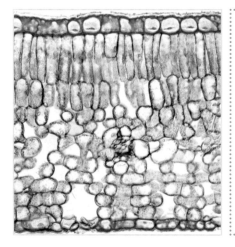

In the space above, make a drawing of what you observe. Add labels to identify four structures. (4)

UpGrade
Many students struggle to identify structures from microscope images. You could make a list of leaf structures and check off each structure when you have labelled it on your drawing.

3 Describe and explain why electron microscopes have greater magnification in comparison to light microscopes. (2)

_____

_____

4 The table below shows some apparatus used to investigate the effect of light on the growth of seedlings. Complete the table by drawing the expected result and give an explanation for your answer.

Treatment	Result	Explanation
thin glass plate separating both sides of the shoot tip	(1)	(2)

5   Scientists investigated the effect of auxin concentration on the angle of growth in seedlings. The table below shows their results.

Concentration of auxin (IAA) / mg/dm³	Estimated angle of growth / degrees
0.05	4
0.10	8
0.15	11
0.20	15
0.25	19
0.30	15

5–1 Plot these results on the graph paper below.   (4)

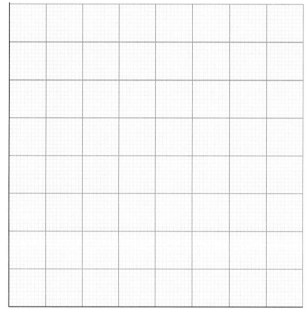

5–2 Give the angle of growth produced at auxin concentration 0.10 mg/dm³.   (1)

_____ degrees

5–3 Explain how the scientist could improve their experiment to determine more accurately the auxin concentration that would cause the maximum angle of growth in the seedlings.   (2)

_____

_____

_____

_____

Mathematics

The questions in this section involve calculations of magnification, real size and image size.

Worked example

1   The image below shows a plant cell. Calculate the magnification of this plant cell.   (3)

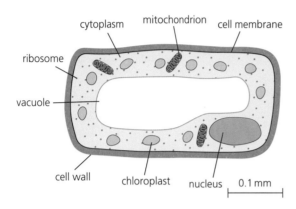

Step 1   *Measure the length of the scale bar.*

15 mm long

Step 2   *Write the formula for magnification.*

$$\text{magnification} = \frac{\text{image size}}{\text{real size}}$$

Step 3   *Calculate the magnification.*

$$\text{magnification} = \frac{15}{0.1}$$

$$\text{magnification} = \times 150$$

Practice questions

2   A plant cell in a photograph measures 12 mm; the actual size of the cell is 80 μm. Calculate the magnification.   (3)

magnification = _____

Insight
It is important to remember the measurements should always be in the same units and so may need to be converted. For example, 1 mm = 1000 μm (micrometres).

3 The actual length of the chloroplast in the image below is 8 µm.

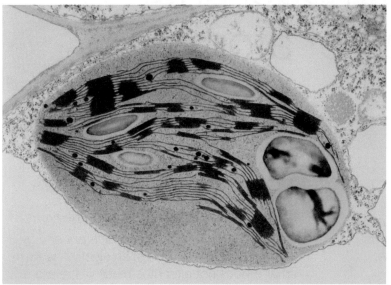

Calculate the magnification. (3)

magnification = _____

4 A plant cell is magnified ×400. The nucleus measures 2.8 mm using the scale bar on the microscope.

4–1 Calculate the actual size of the nucleus. (3)

actual size = _____ µm

4–2 The plant cell is 9 times the length of the nucleus. Estimate the actual length of the plant cell. (1)

_____

4 Atomic model and bonding of atoms

Overview

Knowledge recap

* A substance containing only *one type of atom* is called an *element*. An atom consists of *protons, neutrons* and *electrons*.

* Protons and neutrons make up the *nucleus* and contain the *mass of the atom*. This is the mass number of an element on the periodic table.

* The *atomic (proton) number* is the *number of protons* found in the atom of an element.

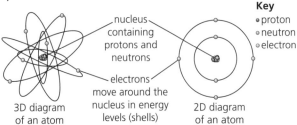

Key
• proton
○ neutron
○ electron

3D diagram of an atom

nucleus containing protons and neutrons

electrons move around the nucleus in energy levels (shells)

2D diagram of an atom

* An *isotope* is a different version of an element. Isotopes have the *same number of protons and electrons* and the *same chemical properties* but *different numbers of neutrons*.

* Electrons *orbit* the nucleus in *different energy levels*. The relative mass of an electron is so small it does not affect the mass of the atom.

* *Relative atomic mass* is the *average mass of all the various isotopes* of that particular element.

* Atoms have an overall charge of 0 as the number of protons (+1 charge) is the same as the number of electrons (–1 charge).

* An *ion* is formed if *electrons are gained or lost*, as the atom becomes *negatively* or *positively charged*.

Practice questions

1 Calculate the number of electrons that are shared in a molecule of oxygen. (1)

_____

_____

UpGrade

Determine the group number(s) of the element(s) that are bonded together. This indicates how many electrons are in the outer shell and therefore how the atoms bond.

2 Draw the electron configuration for Al and for its ion Al^{3+}. (2)

3 Use the information in the periodic table to complete the blanks in the table below. (3)

Atom/ion	Atomic number	Electron configuration
	15	2, 8, 5
K^+		

UpGrade

Use the periodic table to determine which types of elements usually bond together and infer the type of bonding. Metals are on the left-hand side and non-metals on the right.

4 Determine the type of bonding in potassium sulfide and state the chemical formula. (2)

Extended responses

Worked example

1   Over time, the accepted model of the atom has changed considerably. Compare the plum pudding model of the atom and the current model of the atom.   (6)

Plan your answer to this question in the space below. Start by circling the command word and then highlight or underline any useful information. When writing your plan, consider numbering your points in the order you would write them.

Here is a sample answer with expert commentary:

This is not clear enough as the student has used the pronoun 'it' rather than stating which model they are referring to.

This is a confusing sentence as they have identified why the plum pudding model was incorrect, but have contradicted themselves by implying it contains a nucleus.

It was a positively charged ball with bits of negative in random areas. The nuclear model has a positively charged nucleus, where the mass of the atom is. This is surrounded by negative electrons occupying different energy levels. The plum pudding model did not have a nucleus but the atomic model does. The plum pudding model was wrong because the electrons were not surrounding the nucleus, but embedded within the sphere.

This is a good statement about the correct charges of the nucleus and electrons, but it could be improved by stating which subatomic particles make up the nucleus.

This answer would get 3/6 because the student has shown they understand the basic differences between the two models of the atom but has failed to compare in detail or use the correct terminology to specify the subatomic particles.

Be the examiner

2 Diamond and graphite, shown in figures below, are both macromolecules made from carbon. Compare their bonding and structure, and explain how these relate to their respective properties.

(6)

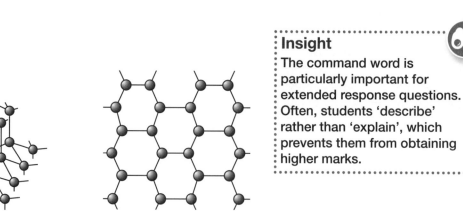

Diamond   Graphite

Read through the sample answer below and comment on what is good and bad about it.

> Graphite and diamond look very different although they are both made from carbon. Diamond is shiny and expensive, whereas graphite is found in pencils. Diamond is a giant covalent structure and each carbon atom is bonded four times. Graphite is bonded covalently but is only bonded three times. Graphite is soft but diamond is hard. Graphite can conduct electricity as it contains delocalised electrons; however, diamond does not conduct electricity.

Use the mark scheme below to help identify how the student did. Use your comments and what you have checked off to give the answer a mark.

Level descriptors	Marks	
Indicative content • Description of diamond as a macromolecule formed from carbon which has covalently bonded four times • Description of graphite as carbon which has covalently bonded three times, forming flat layers • Diamond and graphite both have high melting points due to strong covalent bonds which need to be broken • Graphite conducts electricity as it contains delocalised electrons, but diamond does not • Diamond is very hard as the bonds form a continuous three-dimensional structure • In comparison, graphite is very soft as the layers are held together by weak forces of attraction		☐ ☐ ☐ ☐ ☐ ☐
Level 3: A detailed explanation of both diamond and graphite's bonding and structure is given. Their properties are explained and linked back to how they are bonded. A comparison between the structures must be made. Correct terminology is used throughout.	5–6	☐
Level 2: Explanations are given which clearly state the number of times carbon bonds for diamond and graphite. Student highlights that both structures are bonded covalently. An attempt to compare both structures.	3–4	☐
Level 1: A short description of the number of times carbon bonds for diamond and graphite is given, but there is limited additional information.	1–2	☐

I would give this _____/6 because _____

_____

_____

Practice question

3   Magnesium reacts with fluorine to produce magnesium fluoride, as seen in the equation $Mg(s) + F_2(g) \rightarrow MgF_2(s)$.

Describe the types of bonding in the reactants and explain how the product is formed in terms of electron movement.   (6)

Read through the sample student answer below and make notes on how you would improve it.

Magnesium is a metal, so is bonded metallically and fluorine is a non-metal. Magnesium fluoride is formed when a metal and non-metal react. In this type of bonding electrons move from one atom to the other.

Insight

Examiner reports show that students who use pronouns in longer answers instead of the actual names of compounds or molecules lose out on marks because their answers lack clarity. Make sure you are specific.

Write an improved response to this question that would get full marks.

_____

_____

_____

_____

_____

_____

_____

_____

_____

_____

Practical Chemistry

Practice questions

This question is about the properties of different substances in a chemical reaction. Students often find it difficult to explain how reactants change to form new products, particularly when there are multiple types of chemical bonding involved.

1   When potassium and water react together they produce potassium hydroxide and hydrogen gas as seen in the equation $2K + 2H_2O \rightarrow 2KOH + H_2$.

1–1 Suggest two safety precautions that are needed for the experiment as described. (2)

_____

_____

1–2 Using your knowledge of chemical bonding, state the type of bonding for each reactant and product. (2)

_____

_____

_____

1–3 The potassium reacts to form potassium hydroxide. Explain this reaction both in terms of electron movement and ions formed. (3)

_____

_____

_____

_____

1–4 Draw a dot-and-cross diagram for a molecule of water. (3)

1–5 The experiment was repeated with magnesium instead of potassium. Write out a balanced symbol equation for the reaction. (2)

_____

1–6 Describe and explain the structure and properties of an ionic compound. (3)

_____

_____

_____

This question assesses your knowledge about group 1 metals and their reactions with water.

Exam questions often ask students to compare the electron configuration of each of the group 1 metals and explain how this affects their reactivity.

2   A scientist was given the first three elements in group 1. They wanted to determine which one would give the most vigorous reaction when placed in a water bath.

2–1 Suggest two control variables needed for the experiment as described.   (2)

_____

2–2 Using your knowledge of the group 1 metals and the figure showing electronic configurations of lithium and sodium, explain the patterns in reactivity and determine which chemical would give the most vigorous reaction.   (4)

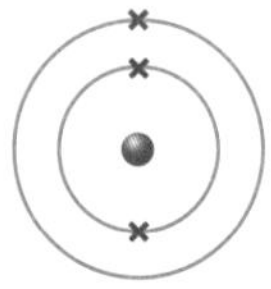

lithium (2, 1)

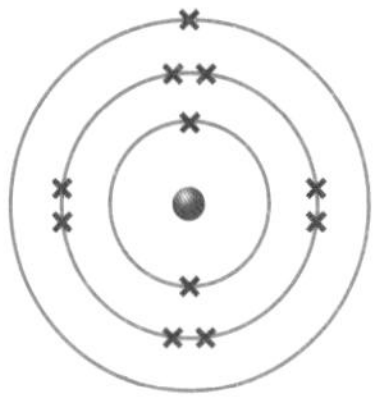

_____

_____

_____

_____

sodium (2, 8, 1)

_____

2–3 Draw the electronic configuration for potassium. State how the electronic configuration relates to the location of potassium in the periodic table.   (3)

UpGrade

To explain trends in reactivity you should always refer to electron configuration and the number of electron shells. As the number of shells increases, there is more shielding around the nucleus.

_____

_____

2–4 Write out a balanced symbol equation for the reaction of sodium with water.   (2)

_____

2–5 Using your knowledge of group 1 metals, explain why the other group 1 metals cannot be used in a school environment.   (2)

_____

_____

_____

Mathematics

The masses of elements on the periodic table are *averages* of the masses of the various *isotopes* which exist and relate to their abundances. The questions in this section will ask you to determine the *relative atomic mass* of different elements, which is a frequent mathematics skill required in Chemistry exams.

Worked examples

1   Isotopes naturally exist in different abundances. Using the table below calculate the relative atomic mass of lithium. Give your answer to two decimal places.   (2)

	Lithium-6	Lithium-7
atomic number	3	3
mass number	6	7
percentage	7.50	92.50

Step 1   *Use the equation.*

$$A_r = \frac{(\text{mass no.} \times \% \text{ of isotope 1}) + (\text{mass no.} \times \% \text{ of isotope 2})}{100}$$

Step 2   *Substitute numbers from the table into the equation.*

$$A_r = \frac{(6 \times 7.50) + (7 \times 92.50)}{100}$$

Step 3   *Show each stage in your working out.*

$$A_r = \frac{45 + 647.50}{100} = \frac{692.50}{100} = 6.925$$

A_r of lithium is 6.93 to two decimal places.

> **Insight**
> Students often don't give their final answer to the right number of decimal places or significant figures. Remember to check what the question asks for.

2   Boron has two main isotopes, B-10 and B-11. The A_r of boron from the periodic table is 10.8. Calculate the percentage of each isotope.   (3)

Step 1   *Use the equation.*

$$A_r = \frac{(\text{mass number} \times a) + (\text{mass number} \times (100 - a))}{100}$$

Step 2   *Substitute numbers into the equation.*

$$10.8 = \frac{(10 \times a) + (11 \times (100 - a))}{100}$$

Step 3   *Show each stage in your working out.*

$1080 = 10a + 1100 - 11a$

$11a - 10a = 1100 - 1080$

$a = 20$

Step 4   *Relate the value back to the question.*

There is 20% of isotope B-10 and 80% of isotope B-11.

Be the examiner

3   Two main isotopes of copper exist, Cu-63 and Cu-65. There is 69.17% Cu-63. Calculate the relative atomic mass of copper. Give your answer to two decimal places. (2)

Insight

Some students lose marks by rounding numbers *before* the end, which can affect calculations and mean the final answer is incorrect.

Looking at the three answers below, work out which one is correct and why the two others are incorrect.

A

$$A_r = \frac{(65 \times 69.17) + (63 \times 30.83)}{100}$$

$= 64.3834$

$= 64.38$ to two decimal places

B

$$A_r = \frac{(63 \times 65) + (69.17 \times 30.83)}{100}$$

$= 62.2751$

$= 62.28$ to two decimal places

C

$$A_r = \frac{(63 \times 69.17) + (65 \times 30.83)}{100}$$

$= 63.6166$

$= 63.62$ to two decimal places

Answer _____ is correct.

Answer _____ is incorrect because _____

Answer _____ is incorrect because _____

Practice questions

4   Two main isotopes of potassium exist. Determine the number of neutrons for each isotope and then use the values in the table below to calculate the A_r. (3)

	Isotope 1	Isotope 2
atomic number	19	19
mass number	39	41
number of neutrons		
percentage	93.3	6.7

_____

_____

_____

5   Two main isotopes of magnesium exist, Mg-24 and Mg-25. There is 78.6% Mg-24. Calculate the relative atomic mass of magnesium. (2)

_____

_____

_____

6   Two main isotopes of chlorine exist, Cl-35 and Cl-37. The A_r of chlorine from the periodic table is 35.5. Calculate the percentage of each isotope. (3)

_____

_____

_____

5 Amount of substance

Overview

Knowledge recap

* The *relative atomic mass (A_r)* is the mass of an atom in comparison to carbon-12. The A_r is an *average* of all the *isotopes* of that element calculated according to their abundance.

* The *relative formula mass (M_r)* is the total of all the relative atomic masses in a compound.

* *Avogadro's constant* is the number of particles in one mole of a substance. This is 6.02×10^{23}.

* To calculate the number of moles, the mass of a substance is divided by its M_r.

* *Conservation of mass* explains that the total mass of the reactants must equal the total mass of the products. When writing chemical equations, the number of atoms on the left and the right of the arrow must also be equal.

* *Atom economy* calculates how much of the reactants becomes the desired product compared to any by-products that form.

$$\text{atom economy} = \frac{M_r \text{ of desired product}}{\text{total } M_r \text{ of all products}} \times 100$$

* The *concentration* of a solution is measured in either g/dm^3 or mol/dm^3. The mass or the number of moles of the solute is divided by the volume of the solution.

Practice questions

1   Write the chemical formula and calculate the relative formula mass (M_r) for calcium hydroxide. (2)

2   Calculate the relative formula mass (M_r) of copper nitrate, $Cu(NO_3)_2$. (2)

3   Write a balanced symbol equation for the complete combustion of butane. (2)

4   An unknown substance has a mass of 1.32 g and is found to contain 0.03 moles. Calculate the M_r of the substance. (1)

5   Calculate the mass of 0.025 moles of carbon dioxide. (2)

Extended responses

Worked example

1 A chemical company carries out the following reaction to produce magnesium hydroxide.

$$MgCl_2 + 2NaOH \rightarrow Mg(OH)_2 + 2NaCl$$

Calculate the atom economy of the reaction. Explain why it is important for companies that the atom economy is as high as possible. (6)

Relative atomic masses (A_r): Mg = 24, Cl = 35.5, Na = 23, O = 16, H = 1

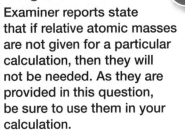

Insight

Examiner reports state that if relative atomic masses are not given for a particular calculation, then they will not be needed. As they are provided in this question, be sure to use them in your calculation.

Plan your answer to this question in the space below. Start by circling the command words, and then highlight or underline any useful information. When writing your plan, consider numbering your points in the order you would write them.

Here is a sample answer with expert commentary:

This is a good sentence as the student has clearly stated the relative atomic masses of the products.

The M_r of magnesium hydroxide is 58 and the M_r of sodium chloride is 58.5. Therefore, the atom economy of the product is [58 ÷ (58 + 58.5)] × 100. This equals 49.8%. It is important that atom economy is high so the company can make more money if the majority of the product is the desired product. The product sodium chloride can be used for other processes.

This is not correct as the student has not referred to the symbol equation when calculating the atom economy.

This is a good sentence as the student has linked the atom economy to economic benefits.

This answer would get 3/6 because the student has correctly calculated the relative atomic masses and stated a reason why atom economy is important. However, the student has incorrectly calculated the atom economy and has not stated that a high atom economy makes the process more sustainable.

Be the examiner

2 Copper is heated to produce copper oxide. Use your knowledge of the conservation of mass to write a balanced symbol equation and plan an experiment the student could do to calculate the mass of oxygen that reacted. (6)

Read through the sample answer below and comment on what is good and bad about it.

> The conservation of mass states that the total mass of the reactants used must equal the total mass of the products formed. The equation for the reaction is $Cu + O_2 \rightarrow CuO$. The student needs to measure the mass of the copper and then place it in a crucible and weigh this. The student needs to heat the crucible with a Bunsen burner. This will cause the reaction to take place and copper oxide to be formed. The mass of the product will be more than the initial mass.

Use the mark scheme below to help identify how the student did. Use your comments and what you have checked off to give the answer a mark.

Level descriptors	Marks	
Indicative content		
• The total mass of the reactants must equal the total mass of the products		☐
• The balanced symbol equation is $2Cu + O_2 \rightarrow 2CuO$		☐
• Weigh the copper metal, then place the copper into a crucible with a lid and weigh both together		☐
• Place the crucible on a clay triangle on a tripod and heat with a Bunsen burner, lifting the lid of the crucible occasionally to allow extra oxygen inside		☐
• Remove the crucible from the heat and weigh again		☐
• The mass after heating should be more than before heating as the copper has reacted with oxygen in the air. Subtract the starting mass from the final mass to calculate the mass of oxygen that was used in the reaction		☐
Level 3: A detailed explanation of the method including equipment required. A balanced symbol equation is included and linked to the conservation of mass. Explanation of the method states that the mass of the reactant and the product need to be measured in order to calculate the total mass of oxygen used in the reaction.	5–6	☐
Level 2: A balanced symbol equation is included and a detailed explanation of the method is given which states that the mass of the reactant and the product need to be measured in order to calculate the total mass of oxygen used in the reaction.	3–4	☐
Level 1: A symbol equation is included and a brief explanation of the method is given which states that the mass of the reactant and the product need to be measured.	1–2	☐

I would give this _____ /6 because _____

_____

_____

Practice question

3   There are two main ways of producing ethanol. One method is hydration of ethane and the other method is fermentation of sugars. Compare and contrast both methods with reference to the reactants needed, the methods and atom economy.

Hydration: $C_2H_4 + H_2O \rightarrow C_2H_5OH$

Fermentation: $C_6H_{12}O_6 \rightarrow 2C_2H_5OH + 2CO_2$ (6)

Read through the sample student answer below and make notes on how you would improve it.

Hydration produces one product, therefore the atom economy is 100%. The atom economy for fermentation is less. Therefore, it is a worse method than hydration. Glucose from sugars is a renewable resource; however, ethane is a non-renewable resource.

Write an improved response to this question that would get full marks.

Practical Chemistry

This section focuses on linking together practical skills with an understanding of variables and balanced symbol equations.

Practice questions

1   Acid rain is a pollutant that is made from the reaction of sulfur dioxide with water. Acid rain can cause damage to limestone buildings. A student wanted to investigate how changing the concentration of an acid affects the rate of a reaction with calcium carbonate.

1–1 For the reaction, the student reacted sulfuric acid with calcium carbonate. Write a balanced symbol equation for the reaction. (2)

_____

_____

1–2 State the independent variable for the reaction and suggest suitable values for this, giving an explanation for your choice. (4)

_____

_____

_____

_____

> **Insight**
> Be sure to say why you chose a specific variable. Examiner reports warn that students often to fail to give valid reasons for their choice of variable when planning an experiment.

1–3 As the student increased the concentration of the sulfuric acid, they noticed the rate of reaction also increased. Explain their results. (3)

_____

_____

_____

_____

> **UpGrade**
> This question links to the topic of reactions. Some questions require you to link knowledge from various topics to show a deeper understanding.

1–4 For each experiment the student used the same volume of acid. Suggest two other control variables. (2)

_____

_____

1–5 For each experiment they used 3 g of calcium carbonate. Calculate the number of moles of calcium carbonate. (2)

_____

_____

2   A scientist carried out a chemical reaction using zinc sulfide and oxygen to produce sulfur dioxide and zinc oxide.

2–1 Write a balanced symbol equation for the reaction. (2)

_____

2–2 Calculate the atom economy of sulfur dioxide in the reaction above. (2)

_____

_____

2–3 Zinc sulfide does not readily react with oxygen. Describe and explain how the scientist gets the reaction to take place. (2)

_____

_____

_____

2–4 The scientist reacted 4.00 g of zinc sulfide in an excess of oxygen. Calculate the maximum theoretical mass of zinc oxide. The scientist only obtained 2.98 g of zinc oxide. Calculate the percentage yield. (4)

Insight
Always include your working. Examiner reports show that students frequently lose marks for not showing clear, easy-to-follow workings.

_____

_____

_____

2–5 Explain why the scientist used an excess of oxygen for the reaction. (2)

_____

_____

2–6 The scientist wants to produce pure zinc from the zinc oxide. Write a method for a displacement reaction. (4)

_____

_____

_____

_____

2–7 Suggest two reasons why the percentage yield is not 100%. (2)

_____

_____

Mathematics

Worked example

This section focuses on calculating the relative formula masses of compounds and creating balanced symbol equations in order to obtain numerical results from experimental data.

1   A scientist burns 11 g of propane in excess oxygen. Calculate the volume of carbon dioxide produced at room temperature and pressure.   (5)

Step 1   *Write a balanced symbol equation.*

$$C_3H_8 + 5O_2 \rightarrow 3CO_2 + 4H_2O \text{ (1)}$$

Step 2   *Calculate the M_r of propane.*

$$(12 \times 3) + (1 \times 8) = 44 \text{ (1)}$$

Step 3   *Calculate the number of moles of propane.*

moles = mass ÷ M_r

moles = 11 g ÷ 44 = 0.25 (1)

Step 4   *Use the molar ratio from the balanced symbol equation.*

1 C_3H_8 : 3 CO_2 therefore 1 : 3 ratio

0.25 moles C_3H_8 × 3 = 0.75

0.75 moles CO_2 (1)

Step 5   *Convert moles of CO_2 to volume.*

One mole of gas at room temperature and pressure occupies 24 dm³.

0.75 × 24 = 18

18 dm³ of CO_2 is produced. (1)

Be the examiner

2   A student reacted excess hydrochloric acid with 25 cm³ of 0.1 mol/dm³ sodium hydroxide to produce a salt and water: $HCl + NaOH \rightarrow NaCl + H_2O$.

Calculate the maximum mass of salt that could be produced. Give your answer to three significant figures.   (3)

Looking at the three answers below, work out which one is correct and why the two others are incorrect.

A

25 cm³ ÷ 1000 = 0.025 dm³

0.025 dm³ × 0.1 = 0.0025

1 : 1 ratio

M_r NaCl = 58.5

0.0025 × 58.5 = 0.14625

= 0.146 g

B

25 cm³ ÷ 100 = 0.25 dm³

0.25 dm³ × 0.1 = 0.025

1 : 1 ratio

M_r NaCl = 58.5

0.025 × 58.5 = 1.4625

= 1.46 g

C

25 cm³ ÷ 1000 = 0.025 dm³

0.025 dm³ × 0.1 = 0.0025

1 : 1 ratio

M_r NaCl = 58.5

58.5 ÷ 0.0025 = 23 400

= 23 400 g

Answer _____ is correct.

Answer _____ is incorrect because _____

Answer _____ is incorrect because _____

5 Amount of substance

40

Practice questions

3   A scientist burns 15 g of pentane in excess oxygen. Calculate the volume of carbon dioxide produced at room temperature and pressure. Give your answer to two decimal places.   (4)

Insight
Examiner reports show students have difficulty writing equations where they have to determine formulae of products. Checking your equation is balanced will help you check if you have deduced the right product.

4   A student has a compound with the empirical formula CH_2O. However, the molecular mass of the compound is 180 g. Calculate the molecular formula and name the compound.   (4)

5   A student reacted excess nitric acid with 20 cm^3 of 0.2 mol/dm^3 sodium hydroxide to produce a salt and water. Calculate the maximum mass of salt that could be produced. Give your answer to three significant figures.   (4)

Overview

Knowledge recap

* A *displacement reaction* is when a metal higher up the reactivity series takes the place of a less reactive metal in a compound.

* Increasing the *temperature of a reaction* causes the particles to have more energy. This causes more successful collisions to occur.

* Increasing the *concentration of reactants* means there are more particles in the same volume, which results in more frequent collisions.

* Increasing the *surface area of the reactants* means there are more exposed particles, which leads to more frequent successful collisions.

* The minimum energy needed for a reaction to occur is called the *activation energy*. This energy is used to break the reactants apart. When products bond, energy is released.

* If the overall energy change (ΔH) is negative, the reaction is *exothermic*. If the energy change is positive, it's *endothermic*.

* *Catalysts* speed up the rate of a reaction by providing an alternative pathway, which reduces the activation energy (E_a).

* Some chemical reactions are *reversible*.

* In a closed system, the *equilibrium* of a reversible reaction can be shifted.

Practice questions

1   Draw a reaction profile for an exothermic reaction with and without a catalyst, clearly labelling the activation energy and overall energy change. (4)

> **Insight**
> Examiner reports show that students often lose marks when drawing reaction profiles. Ensure your diagrams are clear and labelled correctly in order to obtain full marks.

2   When a reversible reaction is at equilibrium, explain why it appears that the reaction has stopped. (2)

3   Describe how changing the pressure in a reversible reaction can change the equilibrium. (2)

Extended responses

Worked example

1   The Haber process is an industrial process that is used to make ammonia. A company wants to make as much ammonia as possible. The forward reaction is exothermic. Use your knowledge of reversible reactions to explain why this process is carried out at 200 atm and 400–450 °C with an iron catalyst.

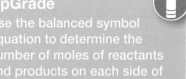

UpGrade

Use the balanced symbol equation to determine the number of moles of reactants and products on each side of the equation.

$$N_2(g) + 3H_2(g) \rightleftharpoons 2NH_3(g)$$ (6)

Plan your answer to this question on a separate piece of paper. Start by circling the command word, and then highlight or underline any useful information. When writing your plan, consider numbering your points in the order you would write them.

Here is a sample answer with expert commentary:

The Haber process is a reversible reaction. Therefore, as the product is being made it forms the reactants again. As hydrogen, nitrogen and ammonia are all gases, the equilibrium can be shifted by changing pressure. The left-hand side of the reaction contains four gaseous molecules, whereas the ammonia is only two molecules. Therefore, increasing the pressure increases the yield of ammonia as the equilibrium moves in the direction to counteract the conditions. A pressure higher than 200 atm is not used as this costs too much because the pipes have to be very strong to withstand the pressure. As the forward reaction is exothermic, to make more ammonia colder conditions are required. However, the process actually occurs at 450 °C. The catalyst does not change the position of the equilibrium but it speeds up the rate of reaction, allowing the ammonia to be made at a faster rate.

This is a good sentence as the student has clearly explained how the equilibrium is shifted, based on Le Châtelier's principle and has stated the correct numbers of molecules from the equation.

This is a good sentence as they have explained why higher pressures are not used, despite producing a greater yield of ammonia.

This part is confusing as, while both statements are correct, they are contradicting each other. The student needs to explain why a high temperature is used.

This answer would get 3/6 because the student has shown they understand how an equilibrium can be shifted by changing the pressure and that there are economic considerations. The student has also explained the importance of the iron catalyst. However, they have not explained why a temperature of 400–450 °C is used.

Be the examiner

2 A student wanted to investigate the effect of changing concentration on rate of reaction. The student reacted calcium carbonate and hydrochloric acid. Plan a method for this reaction, explaining how to ensure it is a fair test, and include the variables. (6)

Read through the sample answer below and comment on what is good and bad about it.

> For this experiment the mass of the calcium carbonate must be the same for each repeat as it is a control variable. The volume of acid also needs to remain the same. For each repeat use a different concentration of acid, for example 0.5 M, 1.0 M and 1.5 M. Measure out 5 g of calcium carbonate and place it in a conical flask, then add the hydrochloric acid. As soon as the reactants are mixed, place the bung and delivery tube on the conical flask which is attached to the gas syringe. Repeat the experiment three times for each concentration of hydrochloric acid.

Use the mark scheme below to help identify how the student did. Use your comments and what you have checked off to give the answer a mark.

Level descriptors	Marks	
Indicative content • Concentration of the hydrochloric acid is changed for each experiment (independent variable) • The dependent variable is the volume of gas collected • Some control variables are the volume of hydrochloric acid, the mass of calcium carbonate and the temperature • In order to make it a fair test the student should repeat each experiment three times • Place the reactants into a conical flask with a bung attached to collect the gas • The student must measure the volume of gas collected at set time intervals (for example every 30 seconds) or measure the volume of gas collected for a set time or until there is no change in volume		☐ ☐ ☐ ☐ ☐ ☐
Level 3: A detailed and safe method which includes repeating the experiment with changing concentrations of acid and clearly identifies all variables. Includes a clear explanation of how to measure the rate of the reaction from the volume of gas collected.	5–6	☐
Level 2: A logical method stating that the experiment must be repeated with changing concentrations of acid and stating some control variables, with an explanation of how to collect the gas.	3–4	☐
Level 1: A simple method stating one variable and explaining that the volume of gas must be measured.	1–2	☐

I would give this _____/6 because _____

_____

_____

Practice question

3   Methane gas can be reacted with steam to produce hydrogen, which is
    needed for the Haber process. Use the chemical equation below to explain
    which conditions would produce the highest yield of hydrogen. The forward
    reaction is endothermic. (6)

$$CH_4(g) + H_2O(g) \rightleftharpoons CO(g) + 3H_2(g)$$

Read through the sample student answer below and make notes on how you would improve it.

> The forward reaction is endothermic, therefore a high temperature will
> increase the yield of hydrogen. Changing the pressure of the reaction
> will also change the position of the equilibrium as all reactants and
> products are gases.

Write an improved response to this question that would
get full marks.

_____

_____

_____

_____

_____

_____

_____

UpGrade

For longer exam questions,
you need to consider all the
conditions and how they affect
the reaction to justify your answer.

Practical Chemistry

This section focuses on the various factors which can alter the rate of reaction and links these to collision theory. It also tests your knowledge on the reactivity series and links together practical skills used for endothermic and exothermic reactions.

Practice questions

1   A scientist reacted 3.0 g of magnesium ribbon with hydrochloric acid in a conical flask. The chemical equation is: $Mg + 2HCl \rightarrow MgCl_2 + H_2$

1–1 Suggest two possible methods for measuring the amount of hydrogen gas that was released. (2)

1–2 The scientist repeated the experiment with 3.0 g of magnesium power. Describe the similarities and differences between the reaction with magnesium ribbon and the reaction with magnesium powder. (2)

> **UpGrade**
> Consider which factors have remained the same and what changed, using this to structure your answer.

1–3 Sketch lines onto the graph below to show the expected results of the following experiments:

   i   Volume of hydrogen gas produced in reaction with 3 g magnesium ribbon

   ii Volume of hydrogen gas produced in reaction with 3 g magnesium powder

   iii Volume of hydrogen gas produced in reaction with 6 g magnesium powder   (3)

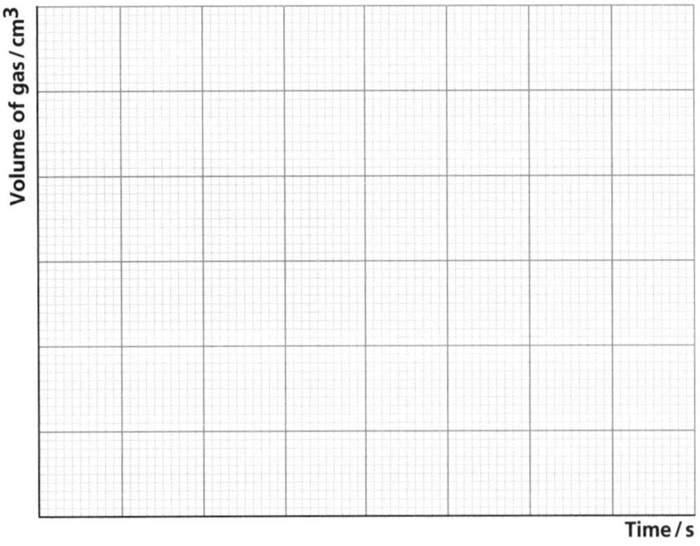

> **Insight**
> When asked to sketch, you only need to draw the overall shape of the graph and do not need to calculate or plot exact values or put scales on the axes.

Volume of gas / cm³ (y-axis), Time / s (x-axis)

1–4 Use collision theory to explain why the rate of reaction changes over time. (4)

1–5 The scientist repeated the experiment but used 1.5 g of magnesium. Describe how this would affect the volume of hydrogen produced. (1)

_____

2 A student wanted to determine the reactivity of some metals. They reacted each metal with a metal sulfate.

2–1 Describe a method the student could follow to carry out the practical. State the control variables. (4)

_____

_____

_____

2–2 They decided not to do three of the experiments and have put a cross in the results table below. Explain why. (1)

	Zinc	Magnesium	Copper	Gold
zinc sulfate	✗			
magnesium sulfate		✗		
copper sulfate			✗	

_____

2–3 Using your knowledge of the reactivity series, complete the table above by placing either a tick or cross in each box to signify if a reaction occurs. (3)

2–4 The reaction between magnesium and copper sulfate is exothermic. Draw and label a reaction profile for this reaction. (4)

2–5 The student wanted to accurately measure the temperature change for this reaction. Outline a brief method, including the equipment needed. (4)

_____

_____

_____

_____

> **Insight**
> When planning a method, you must include the variables. Examiner reports show that while students often include the dependent and independent variables, they often omit the control variables.

Mathematics

This section refers to calculating bond energies in reactants and products and using this information to determine if a reaction is endothermic or exothermic. You also need to be able to calculate the percentage yield of a chemical reaction. The table below states the relevant bond energies needed for the questions in this section.

Bond	Bond energy / kJ	Bond	Bond energy / kJ
N≡N	944	C—H	412
C=O	743	N—H	388
C=C	612	H—Br	366
O=O	496	C—C	348
O—H	463	C—Br	276
H—H	436	Br—Br	193

Worked examples

1   Determine the overall energy change for the complete combustion of propane and state if the reaction is exothermic or endothermic.   (4)

Step 1   *Write a balanced symbol equation.*

$$C_3H_8 + 5O_2 \rightarrow 3CO_2 + 4H_2O$$

Step 2   *Draw displayed formulae of reactants and products.*

Step 3   *Calculate the energy needed to break bonds and the energy released in making bonds.*   (2)

Bonds broken	Bonds made
2 × C—C = 696	6 × C=O = 4458
8 × C—H = 3296	8 × O—H = 3704
5 × O=O = 2480	
Total = 6472 kJ	Total = 8162 kJ

UpGrade

Use the balanced symbol equation to determine how many molecules there are. Multiply this by the bond energy per molecule.

Step 4   *Use the equation.*

overall energy change = bonds broken in reactants – bonds made in product

6472 – 8162 = –1690 kJ

Step 5   *Determine if the reaction is exothermic or endothermic.*

ΔH is –1690 kJ. Therefore the reaction is exothermic. (1)

2 In a reaction, a student calculated that 47.5 g of magnesium chloride when reacted with sodium hydroxide would produce 29 g of magnesium hydroxide. However, the student only obtained 21 g of magnesium hydroxide. Calculate the percentage yield. (2)

Step 1 *Write out the division.*

$$\frac{21}{29} = 0.7241 \ (1)$$

Step 2 *Convert into a percentage.*

$$0.7241 \times 100 = 72.4\% \ (1)$$

Be the examiner

3 In a reaction between calcium oxide and nitric acid, 0.75 g of calcium oxide was used up in 25 seconds. Calculate the mean rate of reaction. (2)

Looking at the three answers below, work out which one is correct and why the two others are incorrect.

A
$$25 \times 0.75 = 18.75 \, \text{g/s}$$

B
$$\frac{25}{0.75} = 33.3 \, \text{g/s}$$

C
$$\frac{0.75}{25} = 0.03 \, \text{g/s}$$

Answer _____ is correct.

Answer _____ is incorrect because _____

Answer _____ is incorrect because _____

Practice questions

4 Bromine water is used to test for alkenes. Propene was reacted with bromine water. Calculate the overall energy change and determine if the reaction is endothermic or exothermic. (4)

_____

_____

_____

_____

_____

5 A student carried out an experiment which produced a yield of 76%. The theoretical maximum mass was 15 g. Calculate the actual mass produced. (2)

_____

_____

6 In a reaction between lithium and hydrochloric acid, 0.5 moles of lithium is used up in 1 minute and 30 seconds. Calculate the rate of reaction. (2)

_____

_____

7 The Earth's atmosphere

Overview

Knowledge recap

* The *early atmosphere* of the Earth was very different to the current atmosphere. Scientists believe that the planet was *extremely hot*, contained *little to no oxygen*, and the surface was covered in many volcanoes. These volcanoes are thought to have released mainly *carbon dioxide*.

* The *oceans* today are thought to have formed from the water vapour in the atmosphere that *condensed* as the temperature decreased.

* The level of *carbon dioxide* has decreased dramatically since the early atmosphere of the Earth. Carbon dioxide has *dissolved into the oceans* as they formed and has been used in *photosynthesis* as plant life evolved.

* The current atmosphere is *approximately 78% nitrogen, 21% oxygen, and 1% other gases*

consisting of *0.9% argon, 0.04% carbon dioxide* and trace amounts of other gases.

* *Greenhouse gases* are found in the atmosphere and are responsible for *keeping the planet warm*. These gases include *carbon dioxide, methane and water vapour*.

* Global warming is the increase in the temperature of the planet and is mainly caused by the increase in greenhouse gases.

* When fuels are burned *atmospheric* can enter the atmosphere. These include *sulfur dioxide, nitrogen oxides, carbon particles, carbon monoxide and carbon dioxide*.

* *Life cycle assessments* are used to determine a product's environmental impact throughout *production, use and disposal*.

Practice questions

1   Explain what is meant by the term *greenhouse gas*.   (2)

_____

_____

_____

2   Describe the effect of sulfur dioxide both on the atmosphere and on humans.   (2)

_____

_____

_____

3   Explain the process that caused the increase in the percentage of oxygen in the atmosphere from the early Earth to the present day. Include a balanced symbol equation.   (4)

> **Insight**
>
> Remember to link changes in gas composition to processes which occurred examiner reports show that students struggle to explain how changes in the Earth's atmosphere came about.

_____

_____

_____

_____

4   Suggest two possible causes for the recent rise in carbon dioxide level.   (2)

_____

_____

5   Describe two environmental concerns associated
    with burning hydrocarbons.   (2)

_____

_____

_____

Insight

Examiner reports show
that students struggle with
environmental concerns around
burning of hydrocarbons.
Ensure you link the pollutant
with the correct effect.

6   Explain the process of carbon capture and storage.   (2)

_____

_____

7   Describe two possible effects of climate change and their cause.   (4)

_____

_____

_____

_____

8   Waste can be disposed of by landfill or by burning. Compare these methods of
    disposal, giving an advantage and disadvantage of each.   (4)

_____

_____

_____

_____

9   State the two nitrogen oxides that are pollutants
    and say how they are formed. Suggest two effects
    of these pollutants.   (4)

_____

_____

_____

Insight

Examiner reports state that
many students are not able to
correctly explain the reactions
between nitrogen and oxygen
which produce nitrogen oxides.
Remember that there is more
than one nitrogen oxide and
learn the chemical formula of
each of them.

_____

_____

Extended responses

Worked example

1   Compare the composition of gases in the Earth's atmosphere from the early Earth to the current atmosphere. Describe and explain how these changes have occurred.   (6)

Plan your answer to this question on a separate piece of paper. Start by circling the command words, and then highlight or underline any useful information. When writing your plan, consider numbering your points in the order you would write them.

Here is a sample answer with expert commentary:

This is a good sentence as the student has followed the command words in the question and compared the carbon dioxide composition in the atmosphere at the two points in time.

The early atmosphere was mainly carbon dioxide; however, there is only 0.04% of carbon dioxide in the current atmosphere. The volcanoes in the early atmosphere released mainly carbon dioxide, meaning a high percentage of the atmosphere was this gas. The carbon dioxide in the current atmosphere is increasing due to deforestation and high volumes of fossil fuels being burned. Oxygen levels have increased; in the early atmosphere there were extremely small quantities of oxygen. However, that has increased to approximately 21% in the current atmosphere. This is because as cyanobacteria and plants have evolved they photosynthesise, which produces glucose and oxygen.

While this statement is correct the student has not answered the question. The student needs to explain why the percentage of carbon dioxide has dropped to 0.04%.

This is a good sentence as the student has explained why the percentage of oxygen has changed.

This answer would get 4/6 because the student has compared the percentages of carbon dioxide and oxygen in the early atmosphere and the present day. The student has also explained why there was a high amount of carbon dioxide in the early atmosphere and how the percentage of oxygen has increased. However, the student has failed to explain why the level of carbon dioxide has decreased, and they have not mentioned any of the other gases in the atmosphere.

7   The Earth's atmosphere

52

Be the examiner

2 The percentage of carbon dioxide in the Earth's atmosphere has risen in recent years. Explain two factors which are causing this rise and the possible effects. Suggest two possible ways to reduce the production of carbon dioxide. (6)

UpGrade
To make your answer more comprehensive, link each factor to how it has caused the carbon dioxide level to rise.

Read through the sample answer below and comment on what is good and bad about it.

The carbon dioxide level is currently rising because lots of fossil fuels are being burned. During the process of complete combustion, the fuel reacts with oxygen and produces carbon dioxide and water. Carbon dioxide is bad as it is a greenhouse gas. This can cause flooding in some areas and droughts in others. Methane is also a greenhouse gas which is caused by cattle being farmed. To reduce the carbon dioxide level, we should burn fewer fossil fuels and use alternative energy sources.

Use the mark scheme below to help identify how the student did. Use your comments and what you have checked off to give the answer a mark.

Level descriptors	Marks	
Indicative content		
• Carbon dioxide levels are rising due to burning fossil fuels as complete combustion produces carbon dioxide		☐
• Carbon dioxide levels are rising because of deforestation. Trees take in the carbon dioxide from the atmosphere for photosynthesis		☐
• Carbon dioxide is a greenhouse gas and absorbs the infrared radiation given off by the Earth, causing the temperature to rise		☐
• An increase in greenhouse gases in the atmosphere can lead to global warming and climate change		☐
• Climate change can:		☐
– cause a change in rainfall		
– cause flooding		
– lead to droughts		
– cause crops to die		
– lead to a loss of habitat for animals		
• The carbon dioxide level can be reduced by burning less fossil fuels and using renewable energy instead, or by replanting more trees		☐
Level 3 A detailed explanation of why the carbon dioxide level is rising, including the burning of fossil fuels and deforestation. An increase in carbon dioxide is linked to global warming and two effects of this are stated. At least one suggestion for how to reduce the level of carbon dioxide is provided.	5–6	☐
Level 2: An explanation of why the carbon dioxide level is rising, including the burning of fossil fuels or deforestation. Two effects of climate change and also one method to reduce the level of carbon dioxide are stated.	3–4	☐
Level 1: The student has stated why the carbon dioxide level is rising and given at least one effect this may cause or stated one way to reduce the carbon dioxide level.	1–2	☐

I would give this _____/6 because _____

_____

_____

Practice question

3 Use the information in the table below and your knowledge of life cycle assessments to evaluate the use of each material to produce bottles. (6)

	Glass bottle	Plastic bottle
raw materials	sand, limestone	crude oil
sustainability	sustainable	not sustainable
manufacture temperature	~1500–1600 °C	~800–900 °C
decompose in landfill	no	no
reusable	yes	no
recyclable	yes	yes

Read through the sample student answer below and make notes on how you would improve it.

> Both glass and plastic bottles have their advantages and disadvantages. We should not use plastic bottles as they are not sustainable. Neither of them will decompose in a landfill, so we should recycle them. Overall glass is better.

Write an improved response to this question that would get full marks.

Practical Chemistry

Fossil fuels are important as when they are burned they produce lots of energy. However, their combustion also produces pollutants which can lead to climate change or cause acid rain. These questions focus on some of these pollutants and their effects.

Practice questions

1   A student burned ethane in the presence of excess oxygen as shown in this equation:

$$2C_2H_6 + 7O_2 \rightarrow 4CO_2 + 6H_2O$$

1–1 Describe and explain a method that would enable the student to collect separately the water vapour and the gas that are produced. (4)

_____

_____

_____

1–2 Write two balanced symbol equations for the possible reactions that could occur if there was not enough oxygen. (4)

_____

_____

_____

1–3 What observations would the student make if incomplete combustion occurred? (2)

_____

_____

_____

1–4 Describe an experiment that the student could carry out to prove that complete combustion had occurred. (3)

_____

_____

_____

2   A student collected two rainwater samples, one from a rural area and the other from a city centre. The student wanted to compare the samples.

2–1 The student added universal indicator to both samples of rainwater. Describe and explain the student's observations. (3)

_____

_____

_____

2–2 The student wanted to determine the effect the rainwater samples have on buildings made of limestone (calcium carbonate). Plan a simple experiment, including any variables, which would allow the student to do this. (5)

_____

_____

_____

_____

_____

_____

2–3 Explain how the pH of the rainwater changes after the addition of the calcium carbonate. (2)

_____

_____

_____

_____

2–4 The student collected the data in the table below. Use the graph below to plot a graph to show the student's results. (4)

Time / s		0	20	40	60	80	100	120	140
Volume of gas collected / cm³	rural rain sample	0	7	13	18	22	25	28	30
	city rain sample	0	12	22	30	36	39	42	43

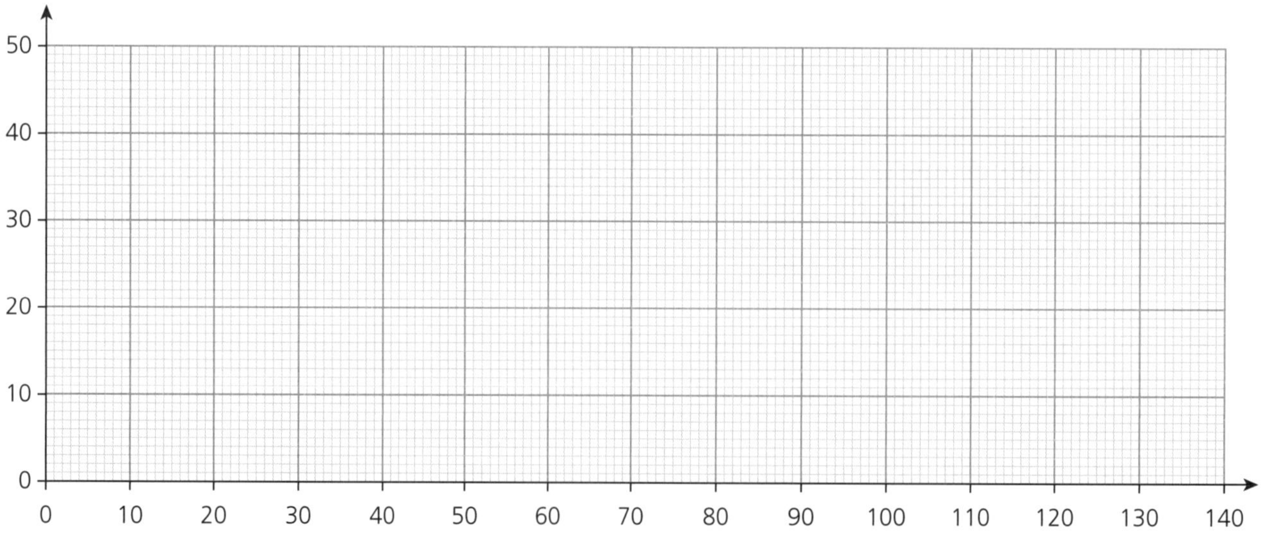

2–5 Explain your choice of graph. (1)

_____

_____

_____

Mathematics

This section focuses on obtaining information from graphs and tables. For data handling questions you need to be able to calculate percentages, extrapolate data and find patterns.

Worked example

1   The Earth's atmosphere has changed considerably from 4.5 billion years ago to the present day. The early atmosphere contained approximately 95% carbon dioxide, whereas the present day atmosphere contains 0.04% carbon dioxide. Calculate the percentage decrease of carbon dioxide. Give your answer to two decimal places.   (3)

Step 1   *Calculate the decrease.* 95 − 0.04 = 94.96 (1)

Step 2   *Divide by original number.* 94.96 ÷ 95 = 0.99958

Step 3   *Multiply by 100.* 0.99957 × 100 = 99.958% (1)

Step 4   *Give your answer to two decimal places.* 99.96% (1)

Practice questions

2   A student wanted to compare the percentages of various gases on the planets closest to Earth, as in the table.

2–1 Calculate the percentage of other gases on Mars.   (1)

	Percentage of gases on the planets		
	Earth	Venus	Mars
carbon dioxide	0.04	96.50	95.00
oxygen	21.00	trace	0.13
nitrogen	78.00	3.50	2.70
other gases	0.96	trace	

2–2 Calculate the percentage difference in nitrogen on Venus compared to Earth. Give your answer to two decimal places.   (3)

3   The percentage of carbon dioxide in the Earth's atmosphere has risen in recent years, as seen in the graph below.

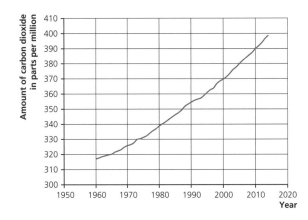

3–1 Use the graph to extrapolate from the data and predict the carbon dioxide level in the atmosphere in 2020.   (1)

3–2 The level of carbon dioxide in the atmosphere in 1980 was 338 ppm. Calculate the percentage increase of carbon dioxide between 1980 and 2010. Give your answer to two decimal places.   (3)

8) Energy

Overview

Knowledge recap

* Energy is the capacity of a physical system to do *work*.

* Energy does not have types but exits in various stores and is measured in Joules, J: chemical, kinetic, gravitational, elastic, thermal, magnetic, electrostatic, nuclear, or vibration.

* If the store is stationary we call it *potential energy*.

* Energy can be transferred usefully, stored or dissipated into the environment as heat, but cannot be created or destroyed.

* Pathways transfer energy at a certain rate which is called *power*, measured in J/s or Watts, W. Energy is transferred by one of the three following energy pathways: as mechanical or electrical work, by heating due to a temperature difference, or by waves as radiation.

* Work done, *W*, is the energy of a force *F* moved through a distance *s*: $W = Fs$ defining 1 J as 1 Nm.

* energy efficiency =
$$\frac{\text{useful energy transfer output}}{\text{total energy transfer input}}$$
power efficiency = $\dfrac{\text{power output}}{\text{power input}}$

* Kinetic energy, $E_K = \frac{1}{2}mv^2$ where velocity = $\dfrac{\text{distance}}{\text{time}}$.

* *Gravitational potential energy, $E_P = mgh$* where *m* = mass in kg, *g* = gravitational field strength, usually taken as 9.8 N/kg or 9.8 m/s^2, and *h* = height in m.

* Force is mass × acceleration ($F = ma$) therefore weight (a force) is mass × acceleration due to gravity.

* *Elastic energy, $E_E = \frac{1}{2}ke^2$* where *k* = spring constant and *e* = the extension of the spring.

* The force applied to a spring = the spring constant × extension.

Practice questions

1   A Mini has a mass of 1175 kg. It is pushed a distance of 3.0 m along the road. Ignoring friction, calculate how much work was done (g = 9.8 m/s^2). Give the unit. (2)

_____

_____

2   The International Space Station orbits at an altitude of 408 km and has a mass of 419 700 kg. Calculate the store of gravitational potential energy. Give your answer to 2 significant figures (g = 9.8 N/kg). (1)

_____

_____

3   A Lamborghini sports car has a mass of 1575 kg and can accelerate from 0 to 60 miles per hour in 2.7 s. A Porsche with the same mass reaches 60 miles per hour in 2.5 s. Explain which is the more powerful car. (3)

_____

_____

_____

Extended responses

Worked example

1 A teacher sets up a large pendulum with a heavy ball suspended on a long rope fixed at the ceiling. The ball is held in front of the teacher's face and then released to swing freely. The teacher keeps perfectly still. Using your knowledge of energy transfers and velocity, and referring to points A, B and C, explain why the ball will not hit the teacher in the face when it swings back. (6)

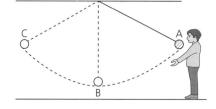

Plan your answer to this question in the space below. Start by circling the command word, and then highlight or underline any useful information. When writing your plan, consider numbering your points in the order you would write them.

> **Insight**
> Examiners report that only around half of students realise that such a ball would not reach the original height it was released from. Consider other real-life situations you may have seen. Energy will always transfer out of a moving system to the surroundings.

Here is a sample answer with expert commentary:

This doesn't make sense. What do they mean by 'more and more negative'? The ball will slow down as it reaches the teacher but that doesn't mean it won't hit.

This is a good point, directly answering parts of the question.

The ball will not hit the teacher in the face because the velocity will become more and more negative, the ball will continue to slow down. The ball starts off with kinetic energy which turns into gravitational potential energy as it falls. At point B the ball is at maximum velocity so has the most kinetic energy. As the ball moves towards point C it loses kinetic energy and gains gravitational potential energy. The velocity at point C is zero and the ball swings back the other way but doesn't get as high because of friction and air resistance.

The student must refer to energy in stores not as types and energy is 'transferred' not 'turned into'.

A correct point about the velocity but again the language of energy transfers needs to be used to explain how friction takes energy away from the pendulum into a heat store of the surroundings.

This answer would score 3/6. The student has mentioned the velocity and energy at two of the three points, B and C, but not in a consistent way. The language of the description of energy transfers is not correct and the reason for friction slowing the pendulum down is not explained.

Be the examiner

2 A cyclist free-wheels down a hill then, at the bottom of the hill, travels along a straight road before applying the brakes and coming to a standstill. Describe and explain the energy transfers that take place including the concepts of *velocity* and *work done*. (6)

Read through the sample answer below and comment on what is good and bad about it.

> The cyclist starts at the top of the hill with gravitational potential energy which is transferred to kinetic energy as the bike speeds up. The bike is at its greatest velocity at the bottom of the hill where it continues at a constant speed until the brakes are applied. The brakes cause friction and slows the bike down until it stops. No work was done as the cyclist didn't pedal.

UpGrade

The concept of energy stores and transfers from them is not well understood by many students. If you refer to a *type* of energy, you will only receive credit if it clearly indicates a store. It is better if you remove the idea of types of energy altogether.

Use the mark scheme below to help identify how the student did and give the answer a mark.

Level descriptors	Marks	
Indicative content		
• A clear story of the transfer of energy from one store to another		☐
• The change in velocity linked to the transfer of energy between potential and kinetic stores		☐
• A description of the bike moving at a steady speed when the potential store is empty but kinetic store is full		☐
• A description of the energy transfers of braking due to friction as work is done by the brakes on the wheels		☐
• A description of the transfer of energy from the kinetic store to a thermal (heat) store in the surroundings (environment)		☐
• An explanation of why the bike slows down (its potential and kinetic stores are empty)		☐
Level 3: A detailed explanation describing energy transfers, clearly referring to energy stores. Link between the change in velocity and the transfer of energy between stores clearly stated. Accurate explanation of the effect of braking and a description of where the energy is transferred to as the bike comes to a stop.	5–6	☐
Level 2: Explanations are accurate but key areas have been missed or don't have enough detail. Mention of the link between the increase of velocity to the increase of energy in the kinetic energy store and a decrease in the potential store. Some explanation of the effect of braking.	3–4	☐
Level 1: Energy stores should be mentioned but if type of energy is mentioned it must be clearly referring to a store. Mentioning of gravitational potential store transferring to kinetic store but answer lacks detail, accuracy or some explanations.	1–2	☐

I would give this ___/6 because _____

_____

_____

Practice question

3   Describe the changes in energy stores as an aircraft takes off, flies a certain distance and then lands.   (6)

Read through the sample student answer below and make notes on how you would improve it.

The aircraft has a full chemical store at take-off. Energy is transferred to a kinetic store as the aircraft speeds up. As the aircraft takes off the gravitational store increases. As the fuel is burned the chemical store empties. When the plane comes into land the gravitational store decreases as does the kinetic store as the plane comes to a stop on the runway.

Write an improved response to this question that would get full marks.

_____

_____

_____

_____

_____

_____

_____

_____

_____

_____

_____

Practical Physics

Practice questions

These questions test ideas around the relationship between force and extension of a spring; the relationship between work done, power and energy stores; and the calculation of efficiency.

1   Hydrogas was an innovative alternative to traditional car suspension systems and was used in British cars from the 1960s to 1990s. Units on each wheel consisted of pressurised spheres containing nitrogen gas that absorbed energy leading to a smoother ride. The compression of one of these units was tested in a lab using various weights giving the following results.

Force / N	Compression / mm
0	0
200	5.0
400	11.5
600	14.0
800	21.0
1000	25.0
1200	26.5
1400	36.0
1600	40.0

UpGrade

When drawing graphs, choose axes that allow you to plot the points you need to over as much of the paper as possible. Always label both axes with title, unit and a regularly spaced number scale.

1–1 Plot the points on the graph paper provided and draw a line of best fit, labelling any outliers. (4)

1–2 Explain how to use the graph to find the spring constant for the hydrogas unit. Calculate the constant, showing your working, and give the unit. (3)

_____

_____

_____

1–3 Calculate the total energy stored in the hydrogas unit when it experiences a force of 1600 N. Describe how you could use the graph to calculate it. (2)

_____

_____

Insight

Examiners report that few students know the unit for the spring constant. Like many units, it is made from the units of the quantities in the formula.

_____

8 Energy

1–4 If the uncompressed hydrogas unit was 180 mm long, calculate its length under a load of 1600 N. (1)

_____

_____

2 When an electrical motor is used to lift a weight, the power supply does work which can be measured with a joulemeter. An experiment was done to see if the efficiency of the motor changed when lifting different weights.

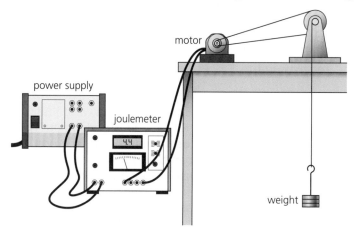

2–1 Explain why the experiment was done three times for each weight. (1)

_____

_____

2–2 Complete the table by calculating the missing efficiencies for each weight. (3)

Weight lifted / N	Energy input Mean / J	Energy output / J	Motor efficiency / %
2	14.3	1.6	11.2
3	20.6	3.2	
4	32.8	4.8	
5	53.3	6.4	
6	74.8	8.0	10.7

2–3 What is the dependent variable in this investigation? (1)

_____

_____

2–4 State why is it important to judge correctly when the weight has reached the top and switch the power supply off promptly. State the name of the kind of error that would be caused if you did not do this. (2)

_____

_____

_____

_____

Mathematics

The questions in this section test your knowledge of rearranging energy equations for kinetic, gravitational and elastic energy stores as well as energy efficiency.

Worked examples

1   Saltburn-by-the-Sea's cliff lift has two cars that run on parallel tracks up the cliff from the pier to the town. Water is pumped into the car at the top until its mass exceeds that of the car at the bottom. The car at the top then slowly descends as the other ascends. If the power output during the 5-minute journey is 1330 W and the car has a total mass of 1100 kg, calculate the height of the cliff ($g = 9.8$ m/s^2). (3)

Step 1   Find the work done: Power $= \dfrac{energy}{time}$ rearranged to $E = Pt$

   $E = 1330 \times (5 \times 60)$ (1) $= 399\,000$ J (1)

Step 2   Equate work done to gravitational potential energy, E_p.

Step 3   Rearrange $E_p = mgh$ to $h = \dfrac{E_p}{mg}$

   $h = \dfrac{399\,000}{1100 \times 9.8} = \underline{37\text{ m}}$ (1)

> **Insight**
> Examiners often warn that not including working out risks losing marks. Partial credit can be given for answers that show equations with correct substitutions even if the final answer is incorrect.

2   A car of mass 1200 kg is travelling at 11 m/s and brakes as it approaches traffic. The car stops in a distance of 20 m. Calculate the force applied by the brakes. (2)

Step 1   Calculate the energy in the kinetic store of the car using $E_K = \dfrac{1}{2}mv^2$. This equals the work the brakes will need to do to stop the car.

   $E_K = 0.5 \times 1200 \times (11)^2 = 72\,600$ J (1)

Step 2   Rearrange $W = Fs$ to give $F = \dfrac{W}{S}$

Step 3   Substitute numbers in: $F = 72\,600 \div 20 = \underline{3600\text{ N}}$ (1)

Be the examiner

3   Gaming console X transfers 1600 J of energy of which 600 J goes into an unwanted heat store. Gaming console Y, which is a similar age, transfers 1200 J of energy and 500 J goes into an unwanted heat store. Calculate which is more efficient. (2)

Looking at the three answers below, work out which one is correct and why the two others are incorrect.

A

X: 600 ÷ 1600 = 0.375

0.375 × 100 = 38%

Y: 500 ÷ 1200 = 0.416

0.416 × 100 = 42%

Y is more efficient.

B

X: 1600 − 600 = 1000

1000 ÷ 1600 = 0.63

Y: 1200 − 500 = 700

700 ÷ 1200 = 0.58

X is more efficient

C

X: 1600 − 600 = 1000

1000 ÷ 1600 = 63%

Y: 1200 − 500 = 700.

700 ÷ 1600 = 44%

X is more efficient.

Answer _____ is correct.

Answer _____ is incorrect because _____

Answer _____ is incorrect because _____

Practice questions

4   At their peak, coal power stations in the UK burned 333 700 kg of coal per day. 1 kg of coal produces 8 kWh of electricity. The UK uses 4.8 kg of uranium per day in nuclear power plants. 1 kg of uranium gives 24 000 000 kWh of energy. Calculate the daily energy output for both types of power station and state which type produced the most energy for the UK per day.   (3)

_____

_____

_____

_____

5   When a load of 10 N is put on a piece of elastic, it extends by 5 cm. Calculate how much energy is in this elastic store.   (2)

_____

_____

_____

6   A 6.0 kg cannonball was taken to the top of the Leaning Tower of Pisa, a point which is 57 m above the ground. Calculate the cannonball's store of gravitational potential energy, and the speed it will reach if dropped to the ground. (Take g = 9.8 m/s^2. Ignore air resistance.)   (2)

> **Insight**
> Examiners report the most common error involving kinetic energy is not realising that the velocity should be squared.

_____

_____

_____

7   An electric motor is used to raise an object with a weight of 20 N. 150 J of energy was supplied to the motor but only 60 J was transferred by it as work done. Calculate the efficiency of the motor.   (1)

> **Insight**
> Efficiency is better expressed as a percentage but examiners may accept a decimal, e.g. 0.5 instead of 50%.

_____

8   Calculate the work done by a person with a mass of 63 kg climbing to the top of the world's tallest building, the Burj Khalifa in Dubai, which is 828 m high. Would eating a chocolate bar that provides 1010 kJ give enough energy for the climb, assuming 100% efficiency? (g = 9.8 N/kg)   (2)

_____

_____

_____

Overview

Knowledge recap

* *Internal energy* is the total sum of the kinetic and potential energies of all the particles in a body. It cannot all be transferred.

* *Thermal energy* is the energy due to a temperature difference. It can be transferred from a body at high temperature to a body with a lower temperature by *conduction* (in solids), *convection* (in fluids and gases) and *radiation* (as infrared).

* A rise in internal energy may not lead to a temperature rise. It may be transferred into intermolecular bonds and lead to a state (or phase) change. This energy is called *latent heat*.

* The energy required to change the state of a substance = mass × specific latent heat, *L*.

* The *specific heat capacity*, *c*, of a substance is the energy required to raise the temperature of 1 kg by 1 °C. The change in thermal energy = mass × specific heat capacity × temperature change.

* Gas pressure is the force of particles on the walls of their container. If the kinetic energy of the particles increases the pressure increases.

* The pressure and volume of a gas are inversely proportional: as volume decreases, pressure increases and vice-versa; pressure × volume = constant.

Practice questions

1   State what a vacuum is. Identify the pressure it exerts on its surroundings.   (2)

_____

2   Explain how the internal energy of a solid just below its melting point increases when it is heated.   (2)

_____

_____

3   A block of expanded polystyrene used in packing material is placed in water. Explain why it will float.   (1)

_____

_____

4   Two students are handed a block of aluminium and a block of wood each. The blocks had been in the classroom all day. One student claims that the aluminium block is colder; the other says this cannot be not the case. Explain why they disagree.   (4)

> **UpGrade**
>
> For something to feel hot or cold there must be an energy transfer due to a temperature difference. Energy will only move if there is this imbalance. Look for temperature difference to decide if there will be a heat transfer.

_____

_____

_____

Extended responses

Worked example

1   A copper rod and a glass rod were held in a Bunsen flame. The copper rod quickly
    became too hot to hold but the glass rod did not. Explain this by comparing the
    transfer of energy from the flame through the copper and the glass.   (6)

Plan your answer to this question in the space below. Start by circling the command word, and then
highlight or underline any useful information. When writing your plan, consider numbering your points in
the order you would write them.

Here is a sample answer with expert commentary:

*This is an unclear
statement; no
explanation has been
given.*

*This is an incorrect
description. The
electrons gain energy
and move faster but
do not vibrate.*

The flame transfers energy by conduction
to the rods. The atoms in the rod start
to vibrate. The copper has free electrons
but the glass doesn't. These free electrons
start to vibrate and move through the
metal hitting other atoms on the way. The
energy from the fast moving electrons
is transferred to the atoms in the metal.
In the glass, each atom transfers energy
to a neighbouring atom without the
electrons to speed up the transfer.

*This is the correct
key word.*

*This is a good comparison
showing that the heat
transfer in the metal has the
advantage of the electrons
as well as vibrating atoms
so heat is transferred quicker
than the non-metal.*

This answer would get 4/6. Conduction was identified but it was not linked to the increased vibration
of atoms. Free electrons were identified but the answer incorrectly states they are vibrating rather than
gaining energy in a kinetic store. Electrons were identified as a factor speeding up the heat transfer.

Be the examiner

2 This vacuum flask is designed to keep liquids at a constant temperature for a period of time. Describe how the features of the vacuum flask keep the liquid inside it hot. (6)

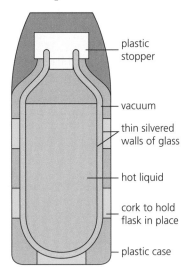

- plastic stopper
- vacuum
- thin silvered walls of glass
- hot liquid
- cork to hold flask in place
- plastic case

Insight
Examiners find that students fail to identify the concept of heat transfer as energy being passed on from one particle to the next via vibrations. Think of heat energy as a particle having *jiggle*. The more *jiggle* it has, the more often that particle will knock into others and the more energy can be transferred on each collision.

Read through the sample answer below and comment on what is good or bad about it.

> The liquid is kept hot because the heat cannot escape very easily from the flask. The plastic stopper stops heat getting out of the top. The silver surface on the glass reflects heat to trap it inside the flask. The cork is an insulator so doesn't let the container get hot so you don't burn your hands.

Use the mark scheme below to help identify how the student did. Use your comments and what you have checked off to give the answer a mark.

Level descriptors	Marks	
Indicative content		
Plastic stopper: • plastic is a poor conductor (or it is an insulator)		☐
• the cap stops energy transfer above the bottle by convection as well as preventing molecules escaping by evaporation		☐
Glass container: • glass is a poor conductor so will reduce energy transfer by conduction		☐
Vacuum: • both conduction and convection require particles so the vacuum stops energy being transferred between the two sides of the glass by conduction and convection		☐
• silvered surfaces reflect infrared radiation / are poor emitters of infrared (heat would be accepted for infrared)		☐
• this prevents energy loss by radiation		☐
Level 3: There are clear explanations of heat-loss prevention from three or more features with simpler statements for at least two more. The processes of conduction, convection and radiation are all mentioned, explained and linked to the correct features.	5–6	☐
Level 2: There is a clear explanation of at least two features with simple statements about others related to mention of correct energy transfers. The prevention of heat transfer by conduction, convection or/and radiation are explained correctly and linked to two features.	3–4	☐
Level 1: A simple explanation of one feature and its role in energy transfer: conduction, convection or radiation is linked correctly to one feature.	1–2	☐

I would give this __/6 because _____

_____

_____

Practice question

3   Explain why gases are easy to compress and what happens to the pressure and the temperature of a gas as it is compressed. (6)

Read through the sample student answer below and make notes on how you would improve it.

> There is lots of space between particles of a gas so it is easy to compress. When a gas is compressed the particles are pushed closer together so they get hot. This means the temperature goes up. The particles move faster and hit the container wall more so the pressure goes up.

UpGrade

Many students simply list the parts in the diagram for answer like this. Your answer needs to explain the heat transfer processes related to each feature.

Insight

Examiners note that students often talk about temperature, pressure, state changes and heat transfers without mentioning molecules (or particles) – a key concept that must be used to achieve full marks.

Write an improved response to this question that would get full marks.

_____

_____

_____

_____

_____

_____

_____

_____

_____

Practical Physics

Practice questions

These questions involve investigating specific heat capacity and latent heat, which are quantities students can confuse.

1   Equipment was set up as below to measure the specific heat capacity of aluminium. Room temperature at the beginning of the investigation was 22 °C.

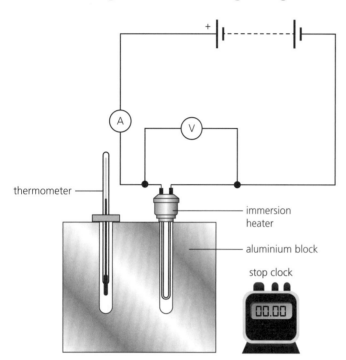

1–1 What is the purpose of using an ammeter and voltmeter in this setup?   (1)

_____

_____

_____

1–2 State the safety considerations when running this investigation.   (1)

_____

_____

_____

UpGrade
When describing heat transfers, be specific about how the heat is transferred.

1–3 Students carrying out this investigation wrapped the aluminium block in a thick layer of bubble wrap packing material. Explain why.   (2)

_____

_____

1–4 The investigation was run for 14 minutes during which the temperature shown on the thermometer went up to 40 °C. The mass of the block was 1.5 kg. The reading on the ammeter was 3 A and the voltmeter read 12 V. Calculate the specific heat capacity of aluminium. Give the correct units.   (4)

_____

_____

_____

1–5 The true value of the specific heat capacity for aluminium is 900 J/kg°C. Calculate the difference between your value and the true value. State whether you think your result is accurate and explain why there could be a difference between the two.   (4)

_____

_____

2 Equipment was set up as below to measure the specific latent heat of fusion of ice.

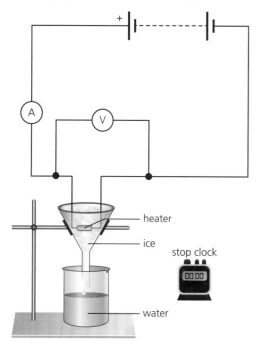

heater
ice
stop clock
water

2–1 State the definition of an independent variable. Identify the independent variable in this investigation. (2)

_____

_____

_____

2–2 State the definition of a dependent variable. Identify the dependent variable in this investigation. (2)

_____

_____

_____

2–3 With the heater switched off, 16 g of water melted in 10 minutes. With the heater switched on, 153 g of water melted in 10 minutes. Calculate the amount of water that the heater melted. (1)

_____

_____

2–4 The readings on the ammeter and voltmeter were 6.4 A and 12 V, respectively. Calculate the latent heat of fusion of the ice. Give the unit. (4)

_____

_____

_____

_____

Mathematics

The questions in this section test your skills in re-arranging more complex formulae.

Worked example

1 Some boiling water is needed to cook spaghetti. A pan is filled with 1.6 kg of cold water at 16 °C and placed on an electric hob that has a power of 3 kW.

1–1 Calculate how long the water will take to boil. (The specific heat capacity of water is 4200 J/kg°C.) (3)

Step 1 *Calculate temperature difference,* $\Delta\theta = 100 - 16 = 84$ °C (1)

Step 2 *Using* $E = m\,c\,\Delta\theta$ *to calculate the energy used:*

$E = 1.6 \times 4200 \times 84 = 564\,480$ J (1)

Step 3 *Rearranging* $E = P\,t$ *to calculate the time taken:*

$$t = \frac{E}{P} = \frac{564\,480}{3000} = 188 \text{ s} = \underline{3 \text{ minutes } 8 \text{ seconds}} \text{ (1)}$$

1–2 Someone questions the accuracy of the previous answer saying it would take much longer to boil the water because the aluminium pan would also have to heat up to 100 °C and transfer its thermal energy via conduction. If the base of the pan has a mass of 400 g and is at a room temperature of 23 °C, calculate how long it would take for it to heat up to 100 °C. Referring to your answer, explain whether the objection is valid or not. (Aluminium has a specific heat capacity of 880 J/kg°C.) (4)

Step 1 $\Delta\theta = 100 - 23 = 77$ °C (1)

Step 2 $E = 0.4 \times 880 \times 77 = 27\,104$ J (1)

Step 3 $t = \dfrac{E}{P} = \dfrac{27\,104}{3000} = 9\text{s}$ (1)

The time for the pan to heat up (9 s) is so much less than the time it takes to heat the water (3 minutes) that it has little effect on the total time taken to bring the water to boil. (1)

Be the examiner

2 A kettle containing 500 g of water was boiled and then left to stand. Energy was transferred from the kettle to the surroundings at a rate of 30 W. Calculate how long the water took to drop to room temperature of 23 °C. (The specific heat capacity of water is 4200 J/kg°C.) (4)

Looking at the three answers below, work out which one is correct and why the two others are incorrect.

A

$E = P\,t$

$t = \dfrac{E}{P} = \dfrac{0.5 \times 4200 \times 23}{30}$

$= 1610\,s = \underline{27 \text{ minutes}}$

B

$500 \times 4200 \times (100 - 23)$
$= 1\,617\,000$ J

$\dfrac{1\,617\,000}{30} = \underline{53\,900\,s}$

C

$100 - 23 = 77$ °C

$E = 4200 \times 0.5 \times 77 = 161\,700$ J

$\dfrac{161\,70}{30} = 5390\,s = \underline{1.5 \text{ hours}}$

Answer _____ is correct.

Answer _____ is incorrect because _____

Answer _____ is incorrect because _____

Practice questions

3 The mass of a gold wedding ring with a volume of 2.072×10^{-7} m^3 is 4.000 g. Calculate the density of the gold in kg/m^3. (1)

> **Insight**
> Examiners' reports show that many students do not give the units for density. Ensure you include the units in the quantities in the formula.

4 Calculate the amount of energy required to melt 20 kg of ice at 0 °C (specific latent heat of fusion of ice = 3.4×10^5 J/kg). (1)

5 A small painted metal figure of a toy soldier of mass 50 g was thought to be made from either silver or lead. When placed in a container of water, the toy soldier displaced 4.4 ml of water. Calculate the density of the soldier and state if it is made from silver or lead (1 litre = 0.001 m^3, the density of silver is 10 500 kg/m^3 and that of lead is 11 400 kg/m^3). (2)

6 A gas has a volume of 8 cm^3 at a pressure of 1.2×10^5 Pa. The pressure was increased to 1.6×10^5 Pa with the temperature unchanged. Calculate the new volume. (2)

7 A kettle of water boils for two minutes transferring 360 000 J of energy. Given the latent heat of vaporisation of water is 2.3 MJ/kg, calculate the mass of water that evaporates in this time. (1)

8 A television studio floor has been covered with a material that can withstand a pressure of 200 kPa. A baby elephant of mass 1020 kg, which has a combined area of its feet of 0.5 m^2, is led in by a presenter wearing high heels with a mass of 50 kg and an area under both feet of 0.0074 m^2. Calculate the pressure of the elephant and of the presenter and state whether either will damage the new floor and why. Take g = 9.8 N/kg. (4)

> **UpGrade**
> g is the acceleration due to gravity on Earth and also the gravitational field strength. It will always be quoted to you as 9.8, 9.81 or sometimes 10. Always use the value for g given in the question.

Overview

Knowledge recap

* *Longitudinal waves* have a vibration in the same direction as the energy transfer.

* *Transverse waves* have a vibration perpendicular to the direction of energy transfer and can be *reflected*, *refracted* or *diffracted*.

* Waves have *amplitude*, *wavelength* (in metres), *frequency* (in Hz) and *speed* (in m/s).

* The wave equation is $v = f\lambda$ (velocity equals frequency times wavelength) where *frequency* is the number of waves that pass a point per second. The time period of a wave is given by $T = \dfrac{1}{f}$.

* Light is an *electromagnetic wave* which can travel through a vacuum and has a spectrum from long-wavelength, low-frequency, non-ionising radio waves through microwaves, infrared and visible light, to short-wavelength, high-frequency, ionising ultraviolet, X-rays and gamma radiation.

* *Seismic waves* are produced by earthquakes. *P-waves* are longitudinal and travel through solid rock and liquid. *S-waves* are transverse and only travel through solid rock.

* Light waves will *refract* (change speed and direction) when they enter a medium of a different density (e.g. air to glass). Water waves will refract when the water changes depth.

Practice questions

1 On the diagram below, label the following: peak, trough, amplitude, wavelength. (3)

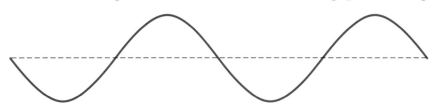

2 Seismic waves can be transverse S-waves or longitudinal P-waves. If the epicentre of an earthquake happens at one side of the Earth, state and explain which of these types of wave can be detected at the opposite side of the Earth. (2)

> **Insight**
> Examiners report that very few students know that S-waves cannot travel through a liquid and relate this to the Earth having a liquid outer core.

_____

_____

3 The waveform shown was recorded by a seismometer over 30 s. Calculate the frequency of these P-waves. (2)

> **Insight**
> In a similar question to this, only 6% gained any marks. Make sure you learn the definition of frequency and its relationship to time as well the wave equation.

_____

_____

Extended responses

Worked example

1   An observer looks over into a dried-up fountain in a park. There is a pile of coins that the observer cannot see from their position. As the fountain is refilled, the coins become visible to the observer.

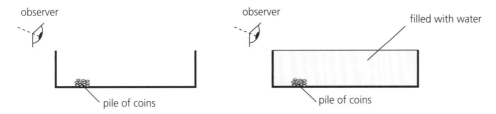

State the name of this phenomenon and explain how the observer can now see the coins. Draw the path of light rays on the second diagram to help your explanation.   (6)

Plan your answer to this question on a separate piece of paper. Start by circling the command word, and then highlight or underline any useful information. When writing your plan, consider numbering your points in the order you would write them.

Here is a sample answer with expert commentary:

The light ray is incorrectly drawn vertically. This would hit the boundary at the normal so no refraction would occur and the line would not change direction.

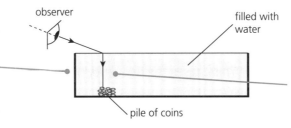

The arrows are the wrong way round. This looks like the light is coming from the eye instead of reflecting off the coins.

The correct name, but always avoid 'it' and define what you are referring to.

It is called refraction. The light slows down when it enters the water causing the light to bend. This is because the water is more dense than air. The light is now bent towards the eye.

This is a true statement but we are concerned here with the light leaving the water not entering it. Use change direction rather than bend.

This is a good description of why refraction happens.

This answer would score 3/6. The knowledge is correct but not clearly described for this case and marks have been lost due to this lack of accuracy. The bending of light rays should always be described by referring to the *normal*, the line perpendicular to the surface being entered by the light. Arrows on light rays should direct from the source to the eye or observer.

Insight

Examiners report large numbers of students cannot identify or draw the normal line. It needs to be drawn perpendicular to the incident surface and included in all diagrams on reflection and refraction.

Be the examiner

2 On 26 December 2004 an earthquake triggered a tsunami sending waves with a speed of 800 km/h towards Indonesia and other countries 250 km away. The waves were initially only 50 cm high but grew to up to 30 m as they reached shallow water. Describe and explain what else changed or did not change as the waves entered the shallower water. Draw wavefronts approaching the island in the shallow water on the diagram. (6)

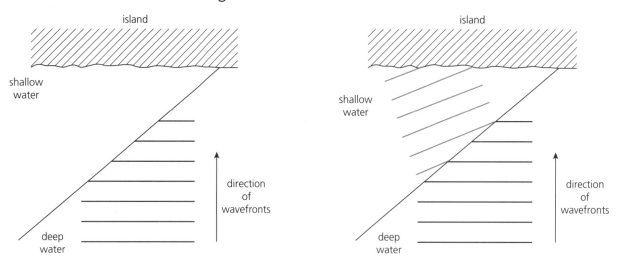

Diagram as provided   Diagram with student additions

Read through the sample answer below and comment on what is good and bad about it.

As the waves entered the shallow water their direction changed due to reflection. This was due to the water being less dense in shallow water. This caused the frequency of the waves to change and their speed decreased as they hit the shore. The wavelength of the waves changed too.

Use the mark scheme below to help identify how the student did. Use your comments and what you have checked off to give the answer a mark.

Level descriptors	Marks	
Indicative content • This is an example of refraction • Waves travel more slowly in shallower water: velocity decreases • The wavelength becomes shorter • The energy and frequency of the waves are unchanged • Straight parallel lines are drawn, connected to the deep-water wavefronts but at a slight anticlockwise angle • The lines are equally spaced, straight and parallel, but closer together than the deep-water lines		☐ ☐ ☐ ☐ ☐ ☐
Level 3: An explanation of refraction due to change in depth. Mention that wave speed (or velocity) is reduced, as is the wavelength. The lines are drawn at an angle, equally spaced but now closer together (shorter wavelength). For full marks, it must state that energy or frequency is unchanged.	5–6	☐
Level 2: Explanations are accurate but key areas have been missed or don't have enough detail. The lines drawn are equally spaced and are at an angle titled anticlockwise from the previous lines, but they may not be closer together. Change of direction is noted and attributed to refraction. Shorter wavelength not noted. Statement that the wave slows.	3–4	☐
Level 1: Parallel lines are drawn, not obviously closer together but equally spaced. Mention of refraction but answer lacks detail, accuracy or some explanations. For example, mention of energy or frequency being unchanged, or wavelength or speed decreasing is missing.	1–2	☐

I would give this ___/6 because _____

_____

_____

Practice question

3   At airports, X-rays are used to examine the contents of suitcases, but microwaves are used to see if people are concealing weapons or banned items on their person. Using your knowledge of the properties of electromagnetic radiation, describe and explain why waves from these parts of the spectrum are used and state any dangers associated with them.   (6)

Read through the sample student answer below and make notes on how you would improve it.

> X-rays are used on suitcases because they can see through most materials so a bomb or gun could be easily seen. You can't use X-rays on people as it could cause cancer. Microwaves can't see through metals but can see through clothes. You can't stand in the microwaves for too long or you will get cooked.

UpGrade

It is important to use the correct terminology. Remember that X-rays are *transmitted* through soft human tissue and less dense materials. They are *absorbed* by bone and metals. The image formed by X-rays is the shadow of the object.

Write an improved response to this question that would get full marks.

_____

_____

_____

_____

_____

_____

_____

_____

_____

_____

Practical Physics

Practice questions

These questions involve investigating transverse waves in water, using a ripple tank, and on a fixed string, using a vibration generator.

1 A ripple tank was set up as shown below.

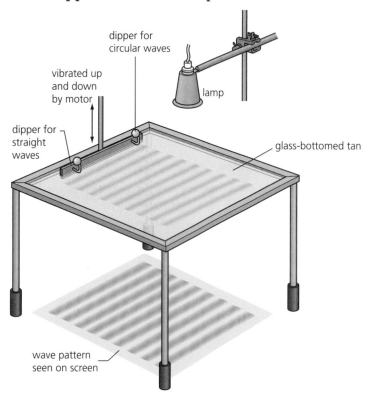

dipper for circular waves

vibrated up and down by motor

lamp

dipper for straight waves

glass-bottomed tan

wave pattern seen on screen

1–1 The voltage supplied to the motor was increased. State what effect this had on the frequency of the waves. (1)

_____

_____

_____

_____

> **Insight**
> Examiners report that only half of students understand frequency is not the same as the wavelength. Note that frequency means *how often* something happens, not how long something is.

1–2 Describe a method to determine the frequency of the waves. (2)

_____

_____

1–3 It is possible to use a ruler to measure the wavelength of waves in a ripple tank. These waves were moving too fast to do that successfully so the teacher suggested using a strobe. Describe how this would help. (3)

_____

_____

_____

1–4 The strobe could not be used so another method was needed. It took 1.5 s for a single wave to travel the 30 cm length of the ripple tank and 960 waves reached the end of the tank in 2 minutes. Use this information to calculate the wavelength of the waves. (3)

_____

_____

_____

2   The equipment below was set up to investigate waves on a string.

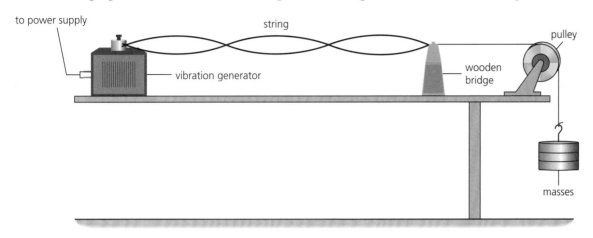

The length of the string from the vibration generator to the wooden bridge was set at 1 m. The height of the waves from peak to trough was measured to be 4.4 cm.

2–1 State what kind of wave was produced. (1)

_____

2–2 Identify what equipment could you use to measure the wavelength of the waves. (1)

_____

2–3 State how many waves are shown in the diagram, and the wavelength. (2)

_____

_____

2–4 Calculate the amplitude of the wave. (1)

_____

_____

2–5 The time period of the wave was 0.02 s. Calculate the wave speed. (2)

_____

_____

_____

2–6 State the effect of having too small a mass and too large a mass on the end of the string. (2)

_____

_____

2–7 State the purpose of the wooden bridge. (1)

_____

_____

Mathematics

The questions in this section test your ability to rearrange the wave equation, to carry out calculations about motion and knowledge and use of standard form.

Worked example

1   Two students stand 8 m apart to demonstrate the motion of a transverse wave on a slinky. The wave has a vertical distance of 32 cm from a trough to a peak, a time period of 0.4 s, and the horizontal distance from a peak to the nearest trough is 48 cm.

Calculate the amplitude, wavelength and speed of the wave.   (4)

Step 1   *Peak to trough = 32 cm. Amplitude is measured from peak to the equilibrium centre point so*

$A = 32 \div 2 = \underline{16 \text{ cm}}$ (or $\underline{0.16 \text{ m}}$) (1)

Step 2   *Wavelength is measured from a point on one wave to the same point on the next.*

It is 48 cm from peak to trough so it is 48 × 2 = 96 cm from peak to peak.

$\lambda = \underline{96 \text{ cm}}$ (or $\underline{0.96 \text{ m}}$) (1)

Step 3   *The time period is 0.4 s.* $f = \dfrac{1}{T} = \dfrac{1}{0.4} = 2.5 \text{ Hz}$ (1)

Step 4   *Using* $v = f\lambda$

$v = 2.5 \times 0.96 = \underline{2.4 \text{ m/s}}$ (1)

Be the examiner

2   An earthquake sets off a tsunami wave which travels at 25 m/s. It has a wavelength of 10 m. The wave is heading towards a deserted island 6 km away. Calculate the frequency of the wave and how many minutes until impact.   (2)

Looking at the three answers below, work out which one is correct and why the two others are incorrect.

A

Frequency = 25 × 10 = $\underline{250 \text{ Hz}}$

Time = 25 × 6 = 150 s

= $\underline{2 \text{ minutes and 30 seconds}}$

B

$f = \dfrac{v}{\lambda} = \dfrac{25}{10} = \underline{2.5 \text{ m/s}}$

$\dfrac{6}{25} = \underline{0.24 \text{ minutes}}$

C

$\dfrac{25}{10} = \underline{2.5 \text{ Hz}}$

$\dfrac{6 \times 10^3}{25} = 240 \text{ s} = \underline{4 \text{ minutes}}$

Answer _____ is correct.

Answer _____ is incorrect because _____

Answer _____ is incorrect because _____

Practice questions

3   A hummingbird beats its wings at a rate of about 70 wing beats per second. The sound wave moves with a velocity of 350 m/s. Calculate the wavelength of the wave.   (1)

_____

_____

4   The highest ocean wave ever recorded was in the Pacific in 1933: it was 34 m high, peak to trough. The wave speed was 23 m/s and the frequency was 0.067 Hz. Calculate the amplitude and the wavelength of the wave.   (2)

_____

_____

5   A red LED has a wavelength of 700 nm (1 nm $= 1 \times 10^{-9}$ m). The speed of light in air is 3.0×10^8 m/s. Calculate the frequency.   (1)

_____

_____

> **UpGrade**
>
> When doing calculations with standard form, the $\times 10^8$ means the number is to be multiplied by 10 eight times so, in this case, it must have 8 zeros after it.
>
> To enter the speed of light on a scientific calculator, press 3 then the [$\times 10^x$] button (on some calculators it is called [EXP] or [EE]) and then enter 8. Pressing [=] will give 300 000 000.

6   A beam of light has a frequency of 6×10^{14} Hz. What colour is the light?   (2)

(The speed of light is 3×10^8 m/s and wavelengths are: yellow = 570–590 nm, green = 495–570 nm, blue = 450–495 nm, violet = 380–450 nm.)

_____

_____

_____

7   Following an earthquake, P waves travel at a speed of 10 km/s and S waves travel at a speed of 4 km/s. Calculate the time difference between the arrival of P and S waves at a seismometer that is 700 km away.   (1)

_____

_____

8   The Beatles album *Sgt Pepper's Lonely Hearts Club Band* ends with a song that has a high-pitched dog whistle. If the speed of sound is 343 m/s and the wavelength of the whistle is 2.28 cm, calculate its frequency.   (1)

_____

9   A microwave oven produces microwaves with a frequency of 6×10^{10} Hz. Calculate their wavelength.   (1)

_____

_____

10 The lowest note on a guitar is the low E string with a frequency of 82.41 Hz. When plucked, the standing wave produced is half a wavelength long and travels at 107 m/s. Calculate the length of the vibrating guitar string from where it is fastened at the neck to the bridge.   (1)

_____

_____

11 Electromagnetism

Overview

Knowledge recap

* Magnets have two poles. Like poles attract, unlike poles repel.

* Magnets can be *permanent* or *induced*. An induced magnet is created by placing a ferromagnetic material in a magnetic field or by passing an electric current through a conductor.

* *Ferromagnetic materials* include iron, steel, cobalt, nickel and some rare earth metals. These are attracted to both poles of a magnet.

* An invisible field surrounds a magnet. It is strongest close to the poles and can be revealed by a *compass needle*.

* A current-carrying wire induces a magnetic field at right angles to the current direction.

* A *solenoid* is a current-carrying coiled wire. When a piece of iron is placed inside the coil it is called an electromagnet. The iron core increases the solenoid's magnetic field.

* The strength of a magnetic field is called magnetic flux density, *B*, measured in Tesla, T.

* The force from an electromagnet is given by the magnetic flux density × current × length: $F = BIL$.

* If a magnet is brought at right angles to a current-carrying wire, the wire will experience a force which will move it at right angles to both the direction of the current and the magnetic field.

* *Fleming's left-hand rule* shows the directions of the force (the thumb), the magnetic field (the forefinger) and the current (middle finger), all at right angles to each other.

* The right hand grip rule shows the direction of the current in a straight wire (the thumb) and the curved fingers as the circular direction of the magnetic field.

Practice Questions

1   The Earth acts like a giant bar magnet. Draw field lines on the diagram below showing the direction of the field, and label the bar magnet inside the Earth with N and S. (3)

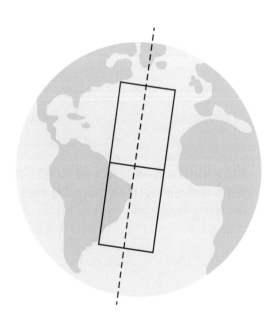

UpGrade
Remember that electric charges and the terminals on a battery are positive and negative, but magnets have poles that are N and S, north and south.

2   Two magnets are placed close together with their north poles facing each other. A non-contact force acts between them. State what is meant by a non-contact force and what the result of that force is.   (2)

_____

_____

3   Some materials become induced magnets when placed in a magnetic field. Tick which three of these materials will not produce an induced magnet.   (1)

Iron ☐   Copper ☐   Steel ☐   Cobalt ☐
Gold ☐   Nickel ☐   Carbon ☐

> **Insight**
> Examiner reports note that students often tick the wrong number of boxes. Always read the question to see how many boxes need ticking.

4   The magnet below was dropped and broke in half. Label the poles on the broken pieces and state what happens if the pieces are pushed closer together.   (2)

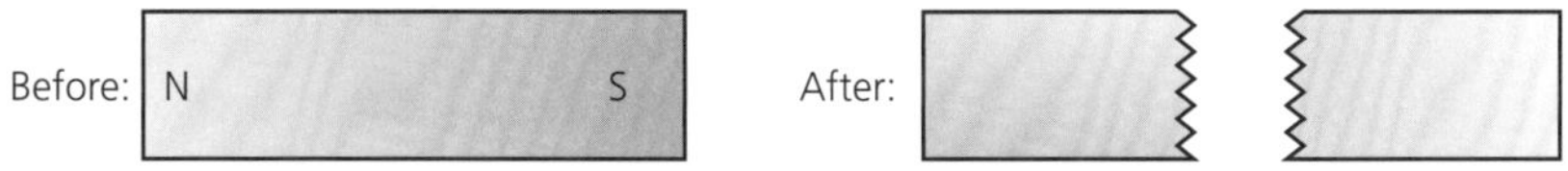

Before: | N   S | After: | ⟩   ⟨ |

5   Fleming's left-hand rule can be used to determine the direction of motion of a current-carrying wire in a magnetic field. State what the following represents: (1)

Second finger

Thumb

First finger: _____

Second finger: _____

Third finger: _____

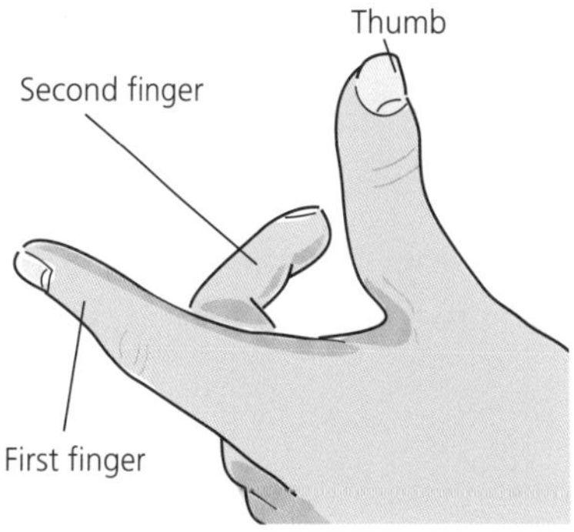

First finger

6   The diagram shows Michael Faraday's first electric motor of 1821. A cell supplies a current which passes around the circuit through the bowl of mercury and the wire. The wire is pivoted so it is able to spin in any direction. A magnet is placed in the bowl. When the switch is closed, the wire hanging down into the mercury spins around the magnet in an anti-clockwise direction.

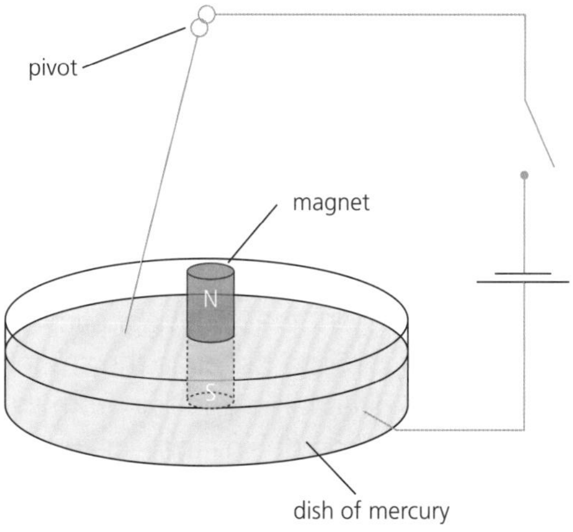

pivot

magnet

N

dish of mercury

6–1 State what happens if:

The polarity of the cell is reversed.   (1)

_____

The magnet is then flipped upside down.   (1)

_____

6–2 State two ways the wire could be made to rotate quicker.   (1)

_____

_____

Extended responses

Worked example

1. A long straight wire is placed vertically through a horizontal piece of card as shown. Describe how this setup can be used to determine the shape and direction of a magnetic field. (6)

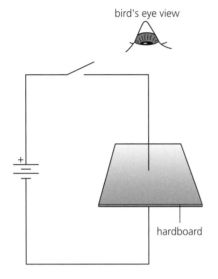

bird's eye view

hardboard

Plan your answer to this question on a separate piece of paper. Start by circling the command word, and then highlight or underline any useful information. When writing your plan, consider numbering your points in the order you would write them.

Here is a sample answer with expert commentary:

This is correct. A strong current will produce concentric circles.

Correct description but see the UpGrade point for clearer language.

> Iron filings can be sprinkled on the card. When the switch is closed the iron filings make a circular pattern around the wire. They are attracted to the magnetic field around the wire, which was created by the current. If a plotting compass is placed near the wire, on the circle of iron filings, the needle will point north giving the direction of the field.

This is a good practical method (but won't help you determine the direction from the diagram).

This answer would get 3/6 because the pattern is described but the key point that the magnetic field is at right angles to the current is missing. No direction has been given for the field because the student has overlooked the right-hand grip rule which could be used to find the direction of the field from the diagram. The use of iron filings has gained a mark, but there is no explanation of why they line up in the way they do.

Be the examiner

2 Relay switches are used in car ignition systems. Describe step by step how the relay switch shown could be used to start a car.

(6)

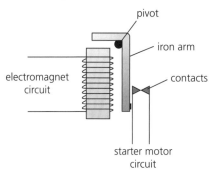

pivot

iron arm

electromagnet circuit

contacts

starter motor circuit

....

Insight

It is important to remember that all magnetic fields are generated by moving charges, and are always at right angles to the direction of the current. Remember: moving charges generate magnetic fields and moving magnetic fields induce moving charges (currents).

....

Read through the sample answer below and comment on what is good and bad about it.

> When the key is turned it supplies electricity to the electromagnet. This means the electromagnet has magnetic charge. The arm pivots making the contacts attract each other making a short circuit so the motor turns on and turns the crank shaft in the engine.

Use the mark scheme below to help identify how the student did. Use your comments and what you have checked off to give the answer a mark.

Level descriptors	Marks	
Indicative content • The key (or switch) completes a circuit to supply current (or electricity) to the electromagnet • The electromagnet produces a magnetic field. It is OK to say it is magnetised or it is 'switched on' • The electromagnet attracts the iron which pivots (or moves) towards it, pushing the contacts together • The contacts are not attracted to each other, they are not magnetised • When the contacts connect, the starter motor circuit is complete • The starter motor then starts the engine		☐ ☐ ☐ ☐ ☐ ☐
Level 3: A detailed step by step description correctly explaining the cause and effect chain that leads to the motor starting up. Knowledge demonstrating that the starter motor is on a different circuit to the ignition key.	5–6	☐
Level 2: Explanation is accurate but key areas have been missed or don't have enough detail. Shows understanding that the electromagnet attracts the iron but lacks detail on the mechanism that closes the contacts.	3–4	☐
Level 1: Mention of the electromagnet becoming magnetic and this having a secondary effect but little or incorrect detail about how the motor starts.	1–2	☐

I would give this _____/6 because _____

_____

_____

Practice question

3   The diagram below shows a d.c. electric motor. Explain why the coil continually moves and whether, in this setup, it will spin clockwise or anti-clockwise.   (6)

Read through the sample student answer below and make notes on how you would improve it.

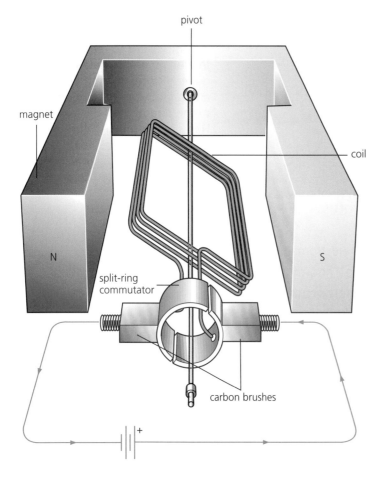

pivot

magnet

coil

N

S

split-ring commutator

carbon brushes

+

> **Insight**
>
> Examiners report that few students understand the key role of the split-ring commutator and how it is essential for the motor to spin. Notice how it maintains electrical contact with the brushes so the coil can spin without tangling wires.

The current in the wire is repelled by the magnet which produces a force at right angles so the coil spins around. When the coil has turned to the other side it is pushed the other way so it keeps spinning. The direction of the coil's spin is given by the left-hand rule and will turn clockwise.

Write an improved response to this question that would get full marks.

_____

_____

_____

_____

_____

_____

Practical Physics

Practice question

This question looks at the relationship between electricity and magnetism, especially the idea that a flow of charge (an electric current) will generate a magnetic field at right angles to it which can then attract magnetic materials or be attracted or repelled by other magnets.

1   A group of students have been asked to build an electromagnet that picks up the greatest number of steel paperclips. They may use any of the following:

•   A power supply capable of supplying 2V to 12V.

•   Some insulated copper wire or some bare copper wire.

•   An iron rod or a steel rod.

1–1 Describe how they could build the strongest electromagnet, explaining the purpose of each piece of equipment chosen.   (6)

_____

_____

_____

_____

_____

_____

_____

_____

1–2 Explain why it could be dangerous to use this electromagnet for a long time.   (2)

_____

_____

_____

1–3 After a few minutes, the power supply suddenly switched off. Another group, who had an identical setup but were using two 6V batteries instead of a power supply, found their electromagnetic did not switch off suddenly. State why the first electromagnet may have switched off and what could be done about it.   (2)

_____

_____

_____

_____

Mathematics

These questions concern re-arranging the formula for the force produced by a current-carrying wire in a magnetic field as well as the use of ratios and proportionality to complete data sets.

Worked example

1 A wire of length 20 cm is placed between the poles of a magnet as shown below.

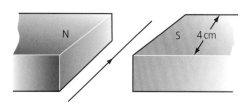

The magnetic flux density is 0.5T and the current is 2.5A. Calculate the force on the wire. (1)

Step 1 *Only the length of wire between the poles of the magnet is relevant.*

Converted to metres, L = 0.04 m.

Step 2 Using $F = BIL$

$F = 0.5 \times 2.5 \times 0.04 = \underline{0.05\,N}$ (1)

Be the examiner

2 A 1 m strip of aluminium foil is clamped vertically and connected in a circuit to a light bulb of resistance 2Ω and a power supply with a potential difference of 12V. When a magnet of width 10 cm is brought near the strip, it flicks away from the magnet driven by a force of 0.6 N. Calculate the magnetic flux density of the magnet. (2)

> **UpGrade**
> Take care entering numbers into a calculator. Use brackets, or work out one part at a time.

Looking at the three answers below, work out which one is correct and why the two others are incorrect.

A

$I = 12 \times 2 = 24\,A$

$B = \dfrac{F}{IL} = \dfrac{0.6}{24 \times 0.1} = \underline{0.25\,T}$

B

$I = \dfrac{V}{R} = \dfrac{12}{2} = 6\,A$

$B = \dfrac{F}{IL} = \dfrac{0.6}{6 \times 0.1} = \underline{1\,T}$

C

$0.6 = B \times \dfrac{12}{2} \times 0.1$

$B = \dfrac{0.6}{\dfrac{12}{2} \times 0.1} = \underline{0.36\,T}$

Answer _____ is correct.

Answer _____ is incorrect because _____

Answer _____ is incorrect because _____

Practice questions

3 A student connected a 5.0 g copper rod to a circuit that provided current of 3.5 A. They lowered the rod between the north and south poles of a strong horseshoe magnet and was surprised to see it floated there. The poles of the magnet were 5 cm apart. Calculate the magnetic flux density of the magnet. Take the gravitational field strength to be 9.8 N/kg. (2)

_____

_____

4   A student made a solenoid by wrapping 300 coils of wire around a plastic tube of circumference 4.0 cm. It was placed between the poles of a magnet from an old speaker that had magnetic flux density 0.30 T and it fitted exactly. When a current of 1.2 A was applied to the coil it moved. Calculate the force that moved the coil. (2)

_____

_____

_____

5   A student created an electromagnet to pick up paperclips.

Turns of wire on the electromagnet	20	30	40	50	60
Number of paper clips picked up	6	9		15	18

The student did not take a measurement at 40 turns of wire. Calculate how many paperclips an electromagnet with 40 turns of wire would be likely to pick up.   (1)

Insight

Examiners note that candidates frequently overlook unit conversion such as cm to m, g to kg, km to m. Always be sure to check the units have been converted to the correct unit before any calculation.

_____

_____

6   An experiment was set up as below. The metal rails were 5 cm apart. When the switch was closed, the reading on the ammeter was 20 A and the brass rod jumped away from the magnet. The magnet was known to have a magnetic flux density of 0.4 T.

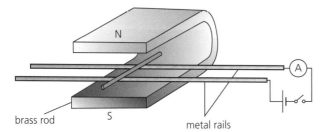

brass rod   S   metal rails

6–1 State the direction the brass rod moved.   (1)

_____

6–2 Calculate the force with which the brass rod moved.   (1)

_____

6–3 The p.d. applied was originally 12 V. It was increased to 24 V. Calculate the current with this new p.d.   (2)

_____

_____

_____

6–4 The rails were moved closer together to 2 cm apart. With the p.d. now at 24 V, state if the brass rod moves with a greater or lesser force than originally.   (1)

_____

Answers

1 Immunity and disease

Overview
Practice questions

1. Heart disease is not an infectious disease as it cannot be transmitted from one person to another (1).

2. Bacteria cause disease by producing toxins which poison and damage tissues and make us feel ill (1). Viruses live and reproduce inside cells which causes damage to cells (1).

3. Antibiotics are only used to treat infections caused by bacteria (1). Malaria is caused by a protist, not a bacterium (1).

4. Preclinical trials test treatments on cells, tissues and animals (1). Clinical trials test treatments on healthy volunteers and patients (1).

5. Malignant tumours are cancerous and invade neighbouring tissues and spread to other parts of the body (1). Benign tumours are contained in one area and do not invade other parts of the body (1).

6. Physical barriers in plants include cellulose cell walls, a tough waxy cuticle on leaves and layers of dead cells around stems (bark on trees) which fall off (2 × examples for 1 mark). Physical barriers in humans include the skin, stomach acid, mucus in the nose, mucus and cilia in the trachea (2 × examples for 1 mark).

7. Vaccines contain dead or weakened forms of pathogens so they can still produce minor symptoms of an illness (1).

8. Monoclonal antibodies are specific to one antigen (1). If this antigen is on the surface of a cancer cell (1) then the monoclonal antibody will only bind to the cancer cell (1), delivering the drug attached to it to the cancer cell and not to other cells (1).

9. The first infection produces specific memory lymphocytes for chickenpox (1). If the chickenpox virus enters the body again, it stimulates these memory cells (1). This results in a faster secondary immune response, preventing the disease developing (1).

10. The answer is incorrect as it is not the disease which enters the phloem, but the pathogen which causes the disease (1). An improved answer would be: 'When a plant contracts tobacco mosaic virus, the pathogen enters the phloem' (1).

Extended responses
Worked example

1. *A model response would be:*

   Monoclonal antibodies are specific to one binding site so can target specific cells and chemicals (1). They are used in detection as they bind to the specific chemical being tested for (1). They are used in pregnancy tests and in labs to detect the levels of hormones and other chemicals in blood, to detect pathogens and to detect specific molecules in cell or tissue samples (1). They are

used in treatment as they bind to specific cancer cells (1), delivering a toxic drug or a chemical which stops cells growing and dividing (1). As they are specific to the cancer cells, they don't harm other cells (1).

Be the examiner

2. *This answer would score 3/6. This answer contains some key omissions. It doesn't mention calculations of area of clear areas, just unspecific measuring; the incubation temperature is incorrect and would not produce valid results; and, apart from incubation time, no other correct control variable is given.*

   A model response would be:

   Soak discs in each of the chemicals to be tested (1). The concentration of chemical on the disc and the diameter of the discs are control variables so should be kept constant (1). Place each disc on a different agar plate which has bacteria growing on it (1). Incubate the plates for 24 hours at 25 °C (1). The incubation time and temperature are also control variables so should be kept constant. After incubation, examine the discs. Any plate containing a disc soaked in a chemical with antibiotic properties would be found to have a clear area around the disc (1). Measure the diameter of the discs and use this to calculate the area of the clear area around the disc. Identify the disc with the largest clear area; this contained the chemical which was the most effective antibiotic (1).

Practice question

3. When people are vaccinated they are given small quantities of dead or inactive forms of a pathogen (1). This triggers an immune response, causing the production of specific antibodies (1) and memory lymphocytes (1). If the same pathogen re-enters the body, the memory lymphocytes are stimulated (1) and the specific antibodies are produced very quickly. This destroys the pathogen and prevents infection (1). If a large proportion of the population is vaccinated, this prevents the spread of disease in a population (1).

Practical Biology
Practice questions

1–1 Patients had to have blood cholesterol above 240 mg/dL which was therefore a health risk (1).

1–2 The pill with no metabolic effect is acting as a placebo (1). It is used as a comparison to make sure that it is the drug being tested which is causing a change in the patient's symptoms (1).

1–3 The drug is effective as the blood cholesterol of each patient decreased (1). The patient whose blood cholesterol was the highest had the biggest decrease (ORA) (1). The drug was not a fully effective treatment as the blood cholesterol of all the patients remained above 240 mg/dL so was still a health risk (1). Use of data from the table, for example, calculate largest fall as 290 – 260 mg/dL (1).

1–4 The fact that patients don't know whether they are being given the placebo or the drug may help reduce bias (1);

however the doctors do know, so this could introduce bias (1). This is therefore not a double-blind trial (1).

2–1 Aseptic techniques are used to prevent contamination of the bacterial samples (1) which could make the results of the investigation invalid (1).

2–2 Flaming the neck of the culture bottle: prevents contamination of the culture bottle by micro-organisms from the environment (1).

Lifting the lid of the agar plate at an angle: prevents contamination of the agar plate by micro-organisms in the air (1).

2–3 1.6×10^4 (2)

2–4 $(15\,600 + 12\,100 + 20\,100)/3 = 15\,933 = \underline{16\,000}$ (1)

2–5 The results seem to have quite a high uncertainty (1) as they have a large range/are not clustered around the mean (1). Use of figures from the table, for example calculation of range $20\,100 - 12\,100 = 8000$ bacteria (1)

2–6 Accuracy is how close the data are to the true value; this cannot be determined by looking at repeats from one experiment (1). The experiment should be repeated with more accurate equipment and the results compared with the results of the original investigation (1).

Mathematics
Practice questions
2 $1.42\,cm = 14.2\,mm$

radius $= 14.2 \div 2 = 7.1\,mm$ (1)

$3.14 \times 7.1^2 = \underline{158\,mm^2}$ (1)

3 Clear area A $= 3.14 \times 49^2 = 7539.14\,mm^2$

Clear area B $= 3.14 \times 45^2 = 6358.5\,mm_2$

Correct area calculations (1)

Percentage difference $= \frac{(7539.14 - 6358.5)}{7539.14} \times 100$ (1)

$= \underline{16\%\ difference}$ (0 d.p.) (1)

2 Hormonal co-ordination in humans

Overview
Practice questions
1 A: thyroid (gland) (1); B: thymus (gland) (1); C: pancreas (1); D: ovary (1)

2 The pituitary gland is called the master gland as it secretes hormones that target other glands such as the thyroid, adrenal, ovaries or testes (1), and in turn causes these glands to release their respective hormones (1).

3

Hormone	Produced by	Target organ	Function
ADH	Pituitary gland	Pancreas (1)	Controls the concentration of water in urine
Insulin	Kidney (1)	Liver	Lowers blood glucose concentration
Oestrogen	Ovaries	Reproductive organs	Controls puberty/ controls the menstrual cycle (1)

4 Osmoregulation is the control of water levels and mineral ions (salt) in the blood (1).

5–1 Anti-diuretic hormone (ADH) (1)

5–2 Pituitary (gland) (1)

5–3 The hormone ADH decreases the volume of urine produced (or results in more concentrated urine) (1). This is because it increases the permeability of the collecting ducts in the kidneys (1), causing more water to be reabsorbed back into the blood (1).

6 A change in the water content of the blood (an increase or decrease in water content of the blood) brings about a corrective mechanism (1). This results in the water content of the blood returning to normal (1).

7–1 *Any two from:*

Produces hormones to control how quickly the body uses energy (1)

Produces proteins (1)

Affects how sensitive the body is to other hormones (1)

Controls metabolic rate (1)

7–2 This is an example of negative feedback control as the level of thyroxine is monitored by the pituitary gland (1). If the level of thyroxine is too low, this causes the pituitary gland to secrete more thyroid-stimulating hormone (TSH) (1). More TSH causes more thyroxine to be secreted and the levels return to normal (1).

7–3 The medication would cause the pituitary gland to release more TSH (or the thyroid gland to release more thyroxine) (1).

7–4 $60 \times 4 = 240\,mg$ (1)

7–5 $240 \div 50 = 4.8$ (1)

$4.8 \times 2.5 = 12\,ml$ (1)

Extended responses
Worked example
1 *A model response would be:*

The water content of the blood is monitored by the osmoregulatory centre (1). When the water content of the blood increases, less ADH (1) is produced by the pituitary gland (1). This causes less water to be reabsorbed by the nephrons and a dilute urine is produced (1). When the water content of the blood decreases, more ADH (1) is produced by the pituitary gland. More water is reabsorbed by the nephrons resulting in a more concentrated urine being produced (1).

Be the examiner
2 *The student would be awarded 4/6 marks because they have correctly explained how the hormones oestrogen and progesterone affect the thickness of the uterine lining. The order of hormone production is also correct, but they forgot to describe that FSH causes an ovum to mature in the ovary. They have also failed to explain the role of LH.*

A model response would be:

The first hormone involved is follicle-stimulating hormone (FSH). FSH causes an ovum in the ovary to mature and causes the ovaries to produce oestrogen (1). The function of the hormone oestrogen is to thicken the lining of the uterus (1). When the levels of oestrogen are high (1), this switches on the release of another hormone called luteinising hormone (LH) (1). LH stimulates an ovum to be released from the ovary;

this is called ovulation (1). The hormone progesterone maintains a thick lining in the uterus if the ovum is fertilised and implants in the lining, in other words, if pregnancy occurs (1).

Practice question

3   Insulin is a hormone produced by the pancreas (1) when the concentration of blood glucose in the body is too high (1). Insulin lowers blood glucose levels (1) by converting glucose to glycogen (1). When the blood glucose concentration falls below normal, the pancreas produces glucagon (1). Glucagon converts glycogen back to glucose which raises blood glucose levels back to normal (1).

Mathematics

Be the examiner

2   Answer B is correct (1). The candidate has calculated the percentage and given their answer to one decimal place (1).

Answer A is incorrect because the percentage should be calculated by multiplying by 100.

Answer C is incorrect because the value for the total amount of blood received (1200 cm³) has been used instead of the value for plasma (700 cm³).

Practice questions

3–1 Axes plotted and labelled (1); appropriate scaling of each axis (1); all plots correct (1)

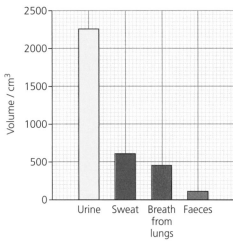

Water lost by the body

3–2 2250 + 600 + 450 + 100 = 3400 (1)

(600 ÷ 3400) × 100 = 17.6% (1)

4–1 The number of people with diabetes in country B increases (1) by 21 107 (1) from 2012 to 2016.

3 Plant structures and hormones

Overview

Practice questions

1   Meristem (1)

2   Active transport (1)

3   Root hair cells have a small thin extension (1) which increases the surface area (1) of the root in contact with the soil. This allows the plant to absorb more water/minerals from the soil (1).

4   Mitochondria have many internal folds which creates a large surface area (1) to increase the rate at which energy is released (1).

5   Root hair cells are found below the soil (1). There is no light for photosynthesis (1).

6   Guard cells (1)

7   *Any two from:* germination; helping plants flower; increasing the size of fruit (2)

8   Xylem is made up from individual cells that have died; phloem cells are living (1).

Xylem cells have no end walls; phloem cells have end walls called sieve plates (1).

Xylem tissue transports water (1); phloem tissue transports glucose/sucrose (1).

9   An organ is a group of tissues that performs a specific function (1). The leaf is made up of xylem tissue, phloem tissue, spongy mesophyll tissue, palisade mesophyll tissue, epidermal tissue, meristem tissue (any two named tissues) (1).

Extended responses

Worked example

1   *A model response would be:*

The upper epidermis is transparent (1). This allows light to pass through to the palisade mesophyll layer (1) for photosynthesis. In the palisade mesophyll layer, cells are tightly packed together which increases surface area (1) for more light to be absorbed for photosynthesis (1). The spongy mesophyll is where gas exchange takes place. The cells are more spherical and have many spaces between them/large surface area in contact with the air spaces (1) to maximise gas exchange (1).

Be the examiner

2   *The student would be awarded 4/6 marks because they have described physical and chemical defences. They have identified both chemical defences and one physical defence. The student failed to explain how the cellulose cell wall acts as a barrier to resist infection by pathogens. In addition, they did not discuss the formation of bark, a layer of dead cells that forms around the stem which falls off, protecting the plant as pathogens fall off with it.*

A model response would be:

Plants defend themselves with physical and chemical responses. Physical defences include a waxy cuticle on the leaves which acts as a barrier to pathogens (1) and cellulose cell walls which act as a barrier to resist infection (1). Another physical defence is bark in trees. This is a layer of dead cells which fall off. When the bark falls off, pathogens also fall off; this protects the plant (1). Plants can produce chemicals to defend themselves. Some produce antibacterial chemicals to prevent bacterial infections (1) or produce chemicals like digitalis to stop them from being eaten (1). Plants may have thorns or spines to prevent them from being eaten (1). This is a form of mechanical defence.

Practice question

3   Measure the length of the seedlings from the seed to the tip of the stalk using the ruler (1) then place

a seedling in the box with a hole cut at the side and place a lamp beside the hole (1). Place another seedling in a box with a hole cut at the top and place under a lamp (1). Then after a set period of time (control factor) I would measure the length of the seedlings and observe the direction of growth for both seedlings (1). In this investigation I would control the distance of the lamps to the seedlings (1) and the size of the hole in the boxes (1) (light intensity/use the same lamp/ temperature would also be accepted as control factors).

Practical Biology

Practice questions

1   Locate the plants cells using the lowest power objective lens (×4) (1). Increase the magnification (×10 or ×40) (1). Use the fine focusing knob to obtain a clearer image (1).

2   Layers are proportionate and representative of photograph (1).

Lines/layers are drawn with smooth lines (1).

Any four labelled structures from: upper epidermis, palisade mesophyll, spongy mesophyll, vascular bundle, xylem, phloem, guard cell, stoma (2)

3   Electron microscopes have a much greater resolution (1) than light microscopes. An electron microscope can resolve points up to 2000 times closer than a light microscope (1).

4

Result	Explanation
Drawing should show seedling growing straight up; no curvature (1)	The glass plate prevents the movement of auxin from the right side to the left side/shaded side to unshaded side (1). The auxin concentration remains the same on both sides so there is even cell elongation (1).

5–1   Concentration of auxin plotted on *x*-axis (1); appropriate scaling of *x*- and *y*-axes (1); units included (1); correct plots joined by a straight line (1)

5–2   8° (1)

5–3   Use smaller concentration/intervals of auxin (1); between 0.20 and 0.30 (1)

Mathematics

Practice questions

2   $12 \times 1000 = 12\,000\,\mu m$ (1)

$\text{magnification} = \dfrac{12\,000}{80}$ (1)

$\text{magnification} = \times 150$ (1)

3   $91 \times 1000 = 91\,000\,\mu m$ (1)

$\text{magnification} = \dfrac{91\,000}{8}$ (1)

$\text{magnification} = \times 11\,375$ (1)

4–1 $\text{actual size} = \dfrac{\text{image size}}{\text{magnification}}$

$2.8 \times 1000 = 2800\,\mu m$ (1)

$\text{actual size} = \dfrac{2800}{400}$ (1)

$\text{actual size} = 7\,\mu m$ (1)

4–2 $7\,\mu m \times 9 = 63\,\mu m$ (1)

4 Atomic model and bonding of atoms

Overview

Practice questions

1   4 electrons (1)

Oxygen (O_2) is double bonded. This means each oxygen atom shares two electrons, so four electrons are shared in total.

2   *1 mark is awarded for a correctly drawn Al electron configuration. 1 mark is awarded for a correctly drawn Al^{3+} electron configuration.*

 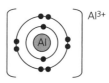

3   *1 mark is awarded for each correct entry in the table.*

Atom/ion	Atomic number	Electron configuration
P	15	2, 8, 5
K^+	19	2, 8, 8

4   It is ionic bonding as potassium is a metal and sulfur is a non-metal (1).

Potassium is in group 1, so has one electron in its outer shell to donate. Sulfur is group 6 so wants to accept two electrons, therefore the chemical formula is K_2S (1).

Extended responses

Worked example

1   *A model response would include any six points from those below. At least one statement from each section must be included:*

The plum pudding model

–   described the atom as a positively charged ball (1)

–   described negatively charged electrons spread throughout the ball (1).

The current model

–   places a positively charged nucleus in the centre of the atom (1)

–   describes the nucleus as made up of protons and neutrons (1)

–   describes the negatively charged electrons as orbiting the nucleus (1)

–   states that these electrons occupy different energy levels (1).

Comparative statements

–   The current model of the atom identifies all three subatomic particles but the plum pudding model only identifies electrons (1).

–   The current model of the atom is mostly empty space, but in the plum pudding model the atom had no empty space (1).

Be the examiner

2   *The student would be awarded 3/6 marks because they have stated how many times both diamond and graphite bond, which is worth 2 marks, but they have not compared the structures. The student gains the third mark for explaining*

why graphite can conduct electricity, with reference to the presence of delocalised electrons.

A model response would be:

Both diamond and graphite are made from covalently bonded carbon atoms. Diamond has a three-dimensional structure where each carbon is bonded four times (1), whereas in graphite each carbon atom is only bonded three times and so there is a layer structure (1). As both macromolecules have strong covalent bonds, which require a lot of energy to be broken, they both have high melting points (1).

The three-dimensional structure in diamond makes it very hard (1), but graphite is made up of layers with weak intermolecular forces of attraction between them (1), which makes it very soft. This is why graphite is often used as a lubricant.

Graphite can also conduct electricity as it contains delocalised electrons which allow current to flow, while diamond does not conduct electricity as it does not have any delocalised electrons (1).

Practice question

3　The reactant magnesium is a metal and is therefore bonded metallically, with the positive metal ions surrounded by delocalised electrons (1).

Fluorine is a diatomic molecule that is bonded covalently (1). Because it is a non-metal, each fluorine atom shares one electron to obtain a full outer shell (1).

The product magnesium fluoride contains ionic bonds (1) as it is a metal and a non-metal bonded together. The metal magnesium donates one electron to become a Mg^+ ion (1) and the fluorine accepts the electron to become a F^- ion (1).

Practical Chemistry

Practice questions

1–1　*1 mark each is awarded for any two from:* students must be standing; goggles must be worn; long hair should be tied back; a safety screen must be used.

1–2　Reactants: K – metallic bonding, H_2O – covalent bonding (1)

Products: KOH – ionic bonding, H_2 – covalent bonding (1)

1–3　Potassium is a metal in group 1 and donates one electron (1) to become a K^+ ion (1). The hydroxide accepts the electron to become a OH^- ion (1).

1–4　*1 mark is awarded for each of the following:*

- Each hydrogen (H) correctly bonded with oxygen (O).
- Two electrons drawn so they are shared in between each hydrogen (H) and the oxygen (O).
- Four other electrons on the shell for oxygen (O).

1–5　*1 mark is awarded for a correct symbol equation and 1 mark for correct balancing:*

$Mg + 2H_2O \rightarrow Mg(OH)_2 + H_2$

1–6　Ionic compounds form ionic lattices (1), which are held together by strong electrostatic forces of attraction (1). It takes a lot of energy to overcome these forces, therefore ionic compounds have high melting and boiling points (1).

2–1　*1 mark each is awarded for any two from:* same mass of each metal; same volume of water; same temperature.

2–2　As you go down group 1 the metals become more reactive, because the shielding increases (1) and the distance from the nucleus to the outer electron also increases (1). The further down the group, the more easily the outer electron is lost (1). Therefore the most reactive metal is potassium (1).

2–3　*1 mark is awarded for a correctly drawn K electron configuration.*

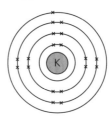

The number of shells indicates the atom's period (i.e. row) in the periodic table: period 4 (1). The number of electrons in the outer shell indicates the atom's group number in the periodic table: group 1 (1).

2–4　*1 mark is awarded for a correct symbol equation and 1 mark for correct balancing:*

$2Na + 2H_2O \rightarrow 2NaOH + H_2$

2–5　The further down group 1, the more reactive the metals become (1). Other group 1 metals would therefore cause a more vigorous reaction which would be unsafe in the classroom (1).

Mathematics

Be the examiner

3　Answer C is correct as the student has multiplied the correct masses and percentages.

$$Ar = \frac{(63 \times 69.17) + (65 \times 30.83)}{100} \quad (1)$$

$$= 63.62 \ (1) \ \text{(rounded to 2 d.p.)}$$

$$\frac{(\text{mass no.} \times \% \text{ of isotope 1}) + (\text{mass no.} \times \% \text{ of isotope 2})}{100}$$

Answer A is incorrect as the student has multiplied the mass of Cu-63 by the percentage of Cu-65 (30.83%), instead of by the correct percentage (69.17%), and vice versa for Cu-65.

Answer B is incorrect as the student has multiplied the masses of Cu-63 and Cu-65 together and multiplied the percentages of each isotope together.

Practice questions

4　*1 mark is awarded for a correctly completed table.*

	Isotope 1	Isotope 2
atomic number	19	19
mass number	39	41
number of neutrons	**20**	**22**
percentage	93.3	6.7

$$A_r = \frac{(39 \times 93.3) + (41 \times 6.7)}{100} \quad (1)$$

$$= 39.13 \ (1)$$

5    $A_r = \dfrac{(24 \times 78.6) + (25 \times 21.4)}{100}$ (1)

     = 24.21 (1)

6    $\dfrac{(35 \times a) + (37 \times (100 - a))}{100} = 35.5$ (1)

     $(35 \times a) + (37 \times (100 - a)) = 3550$

     $35a + 3700 - 37a = 3550$

     $150 = 2a$

     $75 = a$ (1)

     75% Cl-35 and 25% Cl-37 (1)

5 Amount of substance

Overview

Practice questions

1   The chemical formula for calcium hydroxide is $Ca(OH)_2$ (1).

     The relative formula mass of $Ca(OH)_2$ is $40 + 16 + 16 + 1 + 1 = 74$ (1).

2    $NO_3 = 62$ (1)

     $62 + 62 + 63.5 = 187.5$ (1)

     The relative formula mass of $Cu(NO_3)_2$ is 187.5.

3   *1 mark is awarded for a correct symbol equation and 1 mark for correct balancing:*

     $2C_4H_{10} + 13O_2 \rightarrow 8CO_2 + 10H_2O$

     Also accept: $C_4H_{10} + 6.5O_2 \rightarrow 4CO_2 + 5H_2O$

4    $1.32 \div 0.03 = 44$ (1)

5   M_r of $CO_2 = 44$ (1)

     $44 \times 0.025 = 1.1\,g$ (1)

Extended responses

Worked example

1   *A model response would be:*

     The M_r of $Mg(OH)_2$ is 58 and the M_r of NaCl is 58.5 (1).

     The atom economy is $\dfrac{58}{58 + (2 \times 58.5)} \times 100 = 33.14\%$ (1).

     This process is not efficient as the majority of the products are the waste products (1). The higher the atom economy, the more economical the process (1) so a high atom economy makes the process more sustainable (1). Companies try to use the waste products (by-products) for other reactions (1) to reduce the amount of waste.

Be the examiner

2   *The student would be awarded 3/6 marks because they have explained that the mass of the products and reactants must be equal. The student has also given a brief method which explains that the mass must be noted at the beginning and at the end. However, the student has not balanced the symbol equation and they have not identified the specific equipment they would need to carry out the experiment successfully.*

     A model response would be:

     The total mass of the reactants must equal the total mass of the products (1) and this can be seen in the balanced symbol equation: $2Cu + O_2 \rightarrow 2CuO$ (1). This shows that two moles of copper react with one mole of oxygen to produce two moles of copper oxide. To carry out the experiment, the student should weigh the copper metal and then place the copper into a crucible with a lid and weigh these together (1). They should then place the crucible on a clay triangle on a tripod and heat with a Bunsen burner. They should lift the lid of the crucible occasionally to allow extra oxygen inside to ensure a complete reaction (1). Once the reaction has finished, the student should remove the crucible from the heat and weigh it again (1). The mass after heating should be more than before heating as the copper has reacted with the oxygen to form copper oxide. The student should subtract the starting mass from the final mass to calculate the mass of oxygen used in the reaction (1).

Practice question

3   The method of hydration has an atom economy of 100% as there is only one product (1), whereas the atom economy for fermentation is $(92 \div 180) \times 100 = 51\%$ (1). The method of hydration uses ethene which is non-renewable as it is a by-product from crude oil (1). However, fermentation is renewable as it uses sugar from plants (1). Hydration of ethene uses a high temperature and pressure, so it requires a lot of energy (1). Fermentation only requires a warm temperature and a normal pressure (1 atm) so uses little energy (1).

Practical Chemistry

Practice questions

1–1 *1 mark is awarded for a correct symbol equation and 1 mark for correct balancing:*

     $H_2SO_4 + CaCO_3 \rightarrow CaSO_4 + CO_2 + H_2O$

1–2 The independent variable for the reaction is the concentration of the acid (1). The student should use at least three different concentrations of acid (1). They should choose concentrations which are 1.5M or below (1). A concentration above 1.5M is corrosive and a higher risk in a laboratory (1).

1–3 The rate of reaction increases as the concentration increases because there are more reactant particles (1) in the same volume of solution (1). This causes more frequent successful collisions (1).

1–4 *1 mark each is awarded for any two from:* the same mass of calcium carbonate; the same surface area of calcium carbonate; the same starting temperature.

1–5 The M_r of calcium carbonate is 100 (1).

     $3 \div 100 = 0.03$ (1)

2–1 *1 mark is awarded for a correct symbol equation and 1 mark for correct balancing:*

     $2ZnS + 3O_2 \rightarrow 2SO_2 + 2ZnO$

2–2 M_r of $SO_2 = 64$, M_r of $ZnO = 81$ (1)

     atom economy $= \dfrac{2 \times 64}{(2 \times 64) + (2 \times 81)} \times 100 = 44.14\%$ (1)

2–3 Zinc sulfide must be heated in a Bunsen burner for it to react with oxygen (1). This is because energy is required to break the bonds in the reactants (1).

2–4 M_r of $ZnS = 97$, M_r of $ZnO = 81$ (1)

     moles of ZnS $= 4 \div 97 = 0.04$ (1)

     ratio of ZnS : ZnO = 1 : 1

     theoretical mass of ZnO $= 0.04 \times 81 = 3.24\,g$ (1)

     percentage yield $= \dfrac{2.98}{3.24} \times 100 = 91.98\%$ (1)

2–5 An excess of oxygen was used to ensure all the zinc sulfide had reacted (1) and to increase the percentage yield of the products (1).

2–6 Measure out a mass of zinc oxide using a mass balance (1) and place in a test tube. Measure out a set mass of carbon power (1) and add this to the test tube. Turn on a Bunsen burner to a roaring blue flame. Hold the test tube with the reactants in the flame (1). Keep heating until no further change can be seen (1).

2–7 *1 mark each is awarded for any two from*: some reactants are lost during the process; the reaction is incomplete; some reactants are left on the equipment.

Mathematics

Be the examiner

2   Answer A is correct as the student has converted the volume into dm^3 (1) and then multiplied this by the concentration to calculate the number of moles (1). This has then been multiplied by the M_r of NaCl (1).

Answer B is incorrect as the volume has been divided by 100 and not 1000.

Answer C is incorrect as the M_r of NaCl has been divided by the number of moles and not multiplied.

Practice questions

3   $C_5H_{12} + 8O_2 \rightarrow 5CO_2 + 6H_2O$ (1)

M_r of $C_5H_{12} = 72$

$15 \div 72 = 0.208$ moles of C_5H_{12} (1)

ratio of $C_5H_{12} : CO_2 = 1 : 5$

$0.208 \times 5 = 1.04$ moles CO_2 (1)

$1.04 \times 24 = 24.96\,dm^3$ (1)

4   M_r of $CH_2O = 30$ (1)

$180 \div 30 = 6$ (1)

molecular formula $= C_6H_{12}O_6$ (1)

The compound is glucose (1).

5   $HNO_3 + NaOH \rightarrow NaNO_3 + H_2O$ (1)

$20\,cm^3 \div 1000 = 0.020\,dm^3$

$0.020\,dm^3 \times 0.2 = 0.004$ (1)

$1 : 1$ ratio

$M_r\ NaNO_3 = 85$

$0.004 \times 85 = 0.34$ (1)

$= 0.34\,g$ (1)

6 Reactions

Overview

Practice questions

1   *2 marks are awarded for the image below (one with the catalyst, one without the catalyst) and 2 marks for labeling the diagram as shown:*

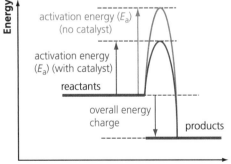

2   When a reversible reaction is at equilibrium, it appears that the reaction has stopped because the forward and backward reactions are both happening (1) at the same rate (1).

3   Increasing the pressure causes the equilibrium to move to the side of fewer molecules (1) and decreasing the pressure causes the equilibrium to move to the side of more molecules (1).

Extended responses

Worked example

1   *A model response would be:*

The forward reaction is exothermic so a lower temperature increases the yield of ammonia (1). However, a lower temperature decreases the rate of reaction (1). Therefore, a temperature of 400–450°C is used as, although it produces a lower yield of ammonia, the rate of reaction is a lot higher (1). A higher pressure would increase the yield of ammonia as there are fewer molecules on the right-hand side of the equation (1). However, a pressure of 200 atm is used as a higher pressure would use more energy/be more expensive (1). A catalyst is used as it speeds up the rate of reaction without being used up itself (1).

Be the examiner

2   *The student would be awarded 4/6 marks because they have correctly identified some control variables and the independent variable. The student has also stated that each concentration should be repeated three times. However, they have failed to explain how often the gas should be collected and that the volume of gas in the dependent variable in this experiment.*

A model response would be:

Weigh out a set mass of calcium carbonate and put it in a conical flask. Then measure out a specific volume of acid and add this to the conical flask (1). The mass of calcium carbonate and the volume of acid need to remain constant as they are control variables (1). Immediately after adding the acid, attach a bung and delivery tube to the conical flask to collect the gas at set time intervals (1). The volume of gas collected is the dependent variable (1). The independent variable is the concentration of the hydrochloric acid, so the experiment needs to be repeated changing this factor (1). To make it a fair test, the student should repeat the experiment three times at each concentration of acid (1).

Practice question

3   The forward reaction is endothermic, therefore a high temperature will increase the yield of hydrogen (1). A high temperature will also increase the rate of reaction (1). The reactants and products are gases, therefore changing the pressure can change the position of equilibrium (1). On the left-hand side of the equation there are two molecules and on the right-hand side there are four molecules (1). To increase the yield of hydrogen a low pressure should be used (1). A catalyst can also be used to increase the rate of reaction (1).

Practical Chemistry

Practice questions

1–1 To measure the amount of hydrogen gas released, the student could use an inverted measuring cylinder in a water bath (1) or a gas syringe (1).

1–2 Magnesium powder has a larger surface area than magnesium ribbon, therefore the gas will be produced more quickly (1). However, both experiments use 3 g of magnesium so the total volume of gas produced will be the same (1).

1–3 *1 mark is awarded for each correct line on the graph:*

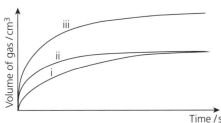

i) Volume of hydrogen gas produced in reaction with 3 g magnesium ribbon

ii) Volume of hydrogen gas produced in reaction with 3 g magnesium powder

iii) Volume of hydrogen gas produced in reaction with 6 g magnesium powder

1–4 At the beginning of the reaction the reaction rate is the fastest (1) as all the particles are reactants so more collisions occur (1). As the reaction progresses, the rate slows down as fewer of the particles are reactants so there are fewer successful collisions (1). The end of the reaction occurs when all of the reactants have formed the products – therefore no collisions can occur (1).

1–5 Using 1.5 g of magnesium instead of 3.0 g of magnesium would produce half the volume of hydrogen gas (1).

2–1 The student should place the metal in a test tube and add the metal sulfate (1), then observe to see if a reaction occurs (1). They should repeat the experiment with the different metals and metal sulfates (1). In the experiment the control variables are the mass of the metals, and the volume and concentration of the metal sulfates (1).

2–2 The student did not do three of the experiments as the metal used is the same as the metal in the sulfate, therefore no reaction would occur (1).

2–3 *1 mark is awarded for each correct row in the table:*

	Zinc	Magnesium	Copper	Gold
zinc sulfate	✗	✔	✗	✗
magnesium sulfate	✗	✗	✗	✗
copper sulfate	✔	✔	✗	✗

2–4 *1 mark is awarded for each of the following:*

- *Correct shape of graph (1)*
- *Reactants and products labelled (1)*
- *Activation energy labelled (1)*
- *Overall energy change labelled (1).*

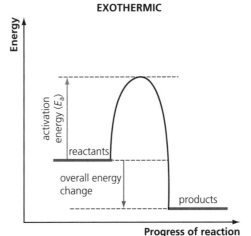

EXOTHERMIC

2–5 The student should measure out the copper sulfate using a measuring cylinder and pour it into a polystyrene cup (1). Then they should add the magnesium to the cup and use a thermometer to record the temperature change as this is the dependant variable (1). They should repeat the experiment at least three times (1) ensuring the mass of the magnesium, volume of copper sulfate and concentration of copper sulfate are the same each time as these are the control variables (1).

Mathematics

Be the examiner

3 Answer C is correct as the mass has been divided by the time $\frac{0.75}{25}$ (1) to give 0.03 g/s (1).

Answer A is incorrect as the mass has been multiplied by the time.

Answer B is incorrect as the time has been divided by the mass.

Practice questions

4 $Br_2 + C_3H_6 \rightarrow C_3H_6Br_2$ (1)

Bonds broken:	Bonds made:
C=C = 612	6 × C—H = 2472
6 × C—H = 2472	2 × C—C = 696
C—C = 348	2 × C—Br = 552
Br—Br = 193	
Total = 3625 kJ	Total = 3720 kJ (1, for each total)

3625 – 3720 = –95 kJ

ΔH is –95 kJ, therefore the reaction is exothermic (1).

5 $\frac{76}{100}$ (1)

$\frac{76}{100} \times 15 = 11.4 \text{ g}$ (1)

6 1 minute 30 seconds = 90 seconds (1)

$\frac{0.5}{90} = 0.0056 \text{ mol/s}$ (1)

7 The Earth's atmosphere

Overview
Practice questions

1. A greenhouse gas is a gas which absorbs infrared radiation from the Earth's surface (1) and emits the infrared radiation causing heat to be trapped in the atmosphere (1).

2. Sulfur dioxide causes acid rain (1) and can cause respiratory problems (1).

3. The process that caused the percentage of oxygen to increase in the atmosphere of the early Earth to the present day is photosynthesis (1). Cyanobacteria (algae) absorbed carbon dioxide and water and produced glucose and oxygen (1).

   1 mark is awarded for a correct symbol equation and 1 mark for correct balancing:

   $$6CO_2 + 6H_2O \rightarrow C_6H_{12}O_6 + 6O_2$$

4. The recent rise in carbon dioxide level is caused by the increase in burning fossil fuels (1) and the increase in deforestation (1).

5. *1 mark each is awarded for any two of:* carbon dioxide is an atmospheric pollutant as it is a greenhouse gas; carbon monoxide is a toxic gas; soot can cause respiratory problems.

6. When fossil fuels are burned, the carbon dioxide can be captured before it is released into the atmosphere by dissolving it in a solvent (1). This solvent is transported deep underground to be stored in rocks (1).

7. *2 marks are awarded for each possible effect of climate change and corresponding cause, up to a maximum of 4 marks:*
   - Sea levels are rising (1) caused by melting ice caps, reducing habitats for animals (1).
   - Some areas are affected by flooding (1) due to the rise in sea levels (1).
   - Food production can be reduced (1) due to flooding or drought, causing crops to be destroyed (1).
   - Loss of animal habitats (1) due to forest fires (1).

8. An advantage of disposing of waste by landfill is that it is economic and materials do not need to be separated (1). However, landfill sites are filling up quickly so there will not be enough space for future waste disposal (1). Burning waste requires less space than landfill (1). However, it does produce carbon dioxide which is a greenhouse gas (1).

9. Nitrogen monoxide (NO) and nitrogen dioxide (NO_2) (1) are formed when nitrogen reacts with oxygen (1). These pollutants can cause acid rain (1) and lead to respiratory health issues (1).

Extended responses
Worked example

1. *A model response would be:*

   The early atmosphere was mainly carbon dioxide. However, the current atmosphere contains only 0.04% carbon dioxide, 78% nitrogen and 21% oxygen (1). Volcanoes released mainly carbon dioxide into the early atmosphere, which led to the high percentage of this gas at that time (1). Over time, the planet cooled, which caused the water vapour released from the volcanoes to condense and form the oceans (1). The amount of carbon dioxide in the atmosphere decreased as it dissolved in the oceans, and algae and plants used it up in photosynthesis (1). Oxygen levels have increased because photosynthesis produces glucose and oxygen (1). The percentage of nitrogen has also changed over time (1).

Be the examiner

2. *The student would be awarded 3/6 marks because they have explained why the carbon dioxide level is rising due to the burning of fossil fuels and have stated two effects of climate change. The student has also given one method to reduce the levels of carbon dioxide. However, the student has not given a second reason for the increase in carbon dioxide levels nor explained the effects of this increase.*

   A model response would be:

   Carbon dioxide levels are rising due to burning fossil fuels – complete combustion produces carbon dioxide (1). Carbon dioxide is a greenhouse gas and absorbs infrared radiation given off by the Earth, causing the temperature to rise (1). Another reason for an increase in the carbon dioxide level is deforestation. Trees take in carbon dioxide from the atmosphere for photosynthesis (1). An increase in greenhouse gases in the atmosphere can lead to global warming and climate change (1). This can cause a change in rainfall patterns, leading to flooding in some areas and droughts in others (1). Carbon dioxide levels can be reduced by burning less fossil fuels and using renewable energy instead, or by halting deforestation and planting more trees (1).

Practice question

3. Bottles can be made from either plastic or glass. Glass bottles are more sustainable than plastic bottles because plastic bottles are made from crude oil, which is a finite resource (1). However, producing glass bottles requires temperatures of 1500–1600 °C, whereas plastic bottles only need temperatures of 800–900 °C (1), so plastic uses less energy in the manufacturing process (1). Neither material will decompose in landfill. However, glass can be reused and recycled (1), whereas plastic cannot be reused but is widely recycled and made into new plastics (1). Overall glass bottles are better as they are more sustainable and can be both reused and recycled (1).

Practical Chemistry
Practice questions

1–1 Carbon dioxide and water vapour are produced during combustion. To collect these products separately, the vapours are passed though sealed glassware (1). The gases pass through a U-tube sitting in a beaker of ice (1) which causes the water vapour to condense and collect, while the carbon dioxide remains a gas (1). The carbon dioxide passes through a delivery tube in a trough of water to be collected in a separate tube as it bubbles up and displaces the water (1).

1–2 *1 mark is awarded for a correct symbol equation and 1 mark for correct balancing:*

   $$2C_2H_6 + 5O_2 \rightarrow 4CO + 6H_2O$$

1 mark is awarded for a correct symbol equation and 1 mark for correct balancing:

$2C_2H_6 + 3O_2 \rightarrow 4C + 6H_2O$

1–3 If incomplete combustion occurred the student would see a smoky flame (1) and a black layer of soot forming (1).

1–4 The student should bubble the gas through limewater (1). If the limewater turns from colourless to a milky colour (1) complete combustion has occurred as this is the test for carbon dioxide (1).

2–1 The sample from the city centre will be acidic and will turn the universal indicator red/orange/yellow (1) as the sulfur dioxide and nitrogen oxides lead to acid rain (1). The rural sample will be less acidic as there is less pollution (1).

2–2 Measure the mass of a piece of limestone and place it in a conical flask, then measure a set volume of rainwater and pour this into the flask (1).

Award marks for either choice of dependent variable (but not both):

- The dependent variable is the change in mass of the limestone (1), so the student must measure the starting mass and final mass to calculate the change in mass in a given amount of time (1).
- The dependent variable is the volume of carbon dioxide produced (1) so the student should attach a gas syringe to the flask and measure the volume of gas produced in a given amount of time (1).

The control variables are the mass and surface area of the limestone and the volume of the rainwater sample (1). These must remain the same when the experiment is repeated with samples of rainwater from different locations.

Location is the independent variable (1).

2–3 The pH of the rainwater before the addition of calcium carbonate is acidic (1). The pH value rises during the reaction with the limestone (1) and becomes less acidic.

2–4 *Marks are awarded for each of the following:*

- Correct labelling of axes – x axis = time (seconds), y axis = volume of gas collected (cm³) (1)
- 8 points plotted correctly (1); all points plotted correctly (2)
- Two lines of best fit drawn (1).

2–5 A scatter graph is used as the independent variable and data collected are both numerical (1).

Mathematics
Practice questions
2–1 $100 - 95.00 - 0.13 - 2.70 = 2.17$ (1)

2–2 $78.00 - 3.50 = 74.50$ (1)

$74.50 \div 78.00 = 0.95513$ (1)

$0.95513 \times 100 = 95.51\%$ (1)

3–1 The level of carbon dioxide in 2020 is predicted to be 410 ppm (accept any value between 408 and 412) (1).

3–2 $390 - 338 = 52$ (1)

$52 \div 390 = 0.1333$ (1)

$0.1333 \times 100 = 13.33\%$ (1)

8 Energy
Overview
Practice questions
1 Use $W = Fs = (1175 \times 9.8) \times 3 = \underline{35\,000}$ (1) Joules, J (1)

2 Use $E_P = mgh = 419\,700 \times 9.8 \times 408 \times 10^3 = 1.7 \times 10^{12}$ J (1)

3 Both cars have the same mass so their kinetic energy ($\frac{1}{2}mv^2$) at 60 mph will be the same (1). Power is the rate at which that energy is delivered. The Porsche delivers the same energy but in a slightly quicker time (1) so it is the most powerful (1).

Extended responses
Worked example
1 *A model response would be:*

The ball will not hit the teacher in the face because as the pendulum swings, energy is transferred as heat – due mostly to friction where the rope is tied and a little to air resistance. Therefore, the height the ball reaches is less and less each swing (1). At point A, the ball is stationary (it has zero velocity) so all its energy is stored as gravitational potential (1). As the ball moves to point B, the energy is transferred into a kinetic store and the ball speeds up (1). It reaches maximum velocity at point B where it has maximum energy in its kinetic store and zero potential (1). As the ball moves to point C, the energy is transferred back into a potential store, which becomes a maximum at point C where the velocity is again zero (1). The ball then falls back, repeating the process (1) until all the energy has been transferred as heat to the surroundings.

Be the examiner
2 *The student would be awarded 3/6. The initial transfer of energy is correct as is the description of acceleration and constant speed. The brakes causing friction earned a mark but the use of work done was incorrect.*

A model response would be:

The cyclist starts at the top of the hill with a maximum energy in their gravitational potential store, which is transferred to a kinetic store as the bike accelerates (1). The bike is at its greatest velocity (with maximum energy in its kinetic store) at the bottom of the hill (1). It continues at a constant speed until the brakes are applied (1). The brakes *do work* on the wheels through friction (1) which transfers energy from the kinetic store to the thermal store of the brake pads and the surrounding air (1). This slows the bike down until all the kinetic energy has been transferred and the bike stops (1).

Practice question
3 The aircraft has a full chemical store at take-off (1). Energy is transferred from this to a kinetic store as the aircraft speeds up, to a gravitational store as it gains height, and to heat stores in the engine and the surrounding air (1). As the fuel is burned, the chemical store empties. When the aircraft descends, the gravitational store decreases, increasing the kinetic store (1). When the aircraft lands, the kinetic store decreases as work is done by the brakes (1), transferring energy into heat stores in the wheels and the environment (1). The plane comes to a stop on the runway with zero energy in the kinetic and gravitational stores, a depleted

chemical store (if some fuel remains) and has increased the thermal store of the environment (1).

Practical Physics
Practice questions
1–1

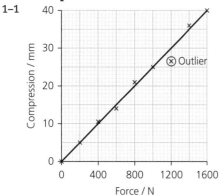

Correct axes (1); points plotted correctly (1); straight line of best fit through the origin (1); outlier at 1200 N labelled (1).

1–2 Calculate the gradient of the straight-line graph by dividing the force by the compression (1)

$1600 \div 40 \times 10^{-3} = \underline{40\,000}$ (1) N/m (1)

1–3 *Using* $E_E = \frac{1}{2}ke^2$

$0.5 \times 40\,000 \times (40 \times 10^{-3})^2 = \underline{32\,J}$ (1)

The energy stored is the area under the graph (1) which is half of force × compression.

If you rearrange $F = ke$ *to get* $k = F/e$ *and substitute that into* $E_E = \frac{1}{2}ke^2$, *you get* $E_E = \frac{1}{2}Fe$.

1–4 $180 - 40 = \underline{140\,mm}$ (1)

2–1 To increase reliability (1). *Do not accept simply 'to calculate the mean (or average)'.*

2–2 *1 mark for each correct bold number.*

Weight lifted / N	Mean energy input / J	Energy output / J	Motor efficiency / %
2	14.3	1.6	11.2
3	20.6	3.2	**15.5**
4	32.8	4.8	**14.6**
5	53.3	6.4	**12.0**
6	74.8	8.0	10.7

2–3 The joulemeter reading of energy (1).

2–4 The joulemeter would record that more energy had been used than was needed (1). This would be a systematic error (1).

Mathematics
Be the examiner
3 Answer B is correct even though the answers have not been converted to percentages. The unwanted energy was subtracted from the input to find the useful energy (1). Then that was divided by the total input to get the correct answer (1).

Answer A is incorrect because the unwanted energy store (heat) has been used instead of the useful energy.

Answer C is incorrect because the input energy for the gaming console X has been used by mistake in the gaming console Y calculation.

Practice questions
4 Coal: $333\,700 \times 8 = \underline{2.7 \times 10^6\,kWh\,per\,day}$ (1)

Nuclear: $24\,000\,000 \times 4.8 = \underline{1.2 \times 10^8\,kWh\,per\,day}$ (1) – the most (1).

5 Rearrange $F = ke$ to give $k = \dfrac{F}{e} = \dfrac{10}{0.05} = 200$ N/m (1)

Use $E_E = \frac{1}{2}ke^2 = 0.5 \times 200 \times (0.05)^2 = \underline{0.25\,J}$ (1)

6 $E_P = mgh = 6.0 \times 9.8 \times 57 = \underline{3351.6\,J}$ (1)

Use $E_P = E_K = \frac{1}{2}mv^2$ rearranged to $v^2 = \dfrac{2E_K}{m} = 1117.2$

$\Rightarrow v = \underline{33\,m/s}$ (1)

7 Efficiency $= \dfrac{\text{enegry transferred}}{\text{enegry supplied}} = \dfrac{60}{150} = \underline{40\%}$ (1)

8 Work done $= mgh = 63 \times 9.8 \times 828 = \underline{510\,000\,J}$ (1)

1010 kJ is nearly twice the amount needed (1) or only half a bar is needed because 510 000 J is around half of 1010 kJ (1).

9 Particle theory

Overview
Practice questions
1 A volume of space that contains few or no particles (1) resulting in little or no pressure (1).

2 The energy supplied increases the internal energy of the material. It is at first transferred to a potential energy store in the bonds between the molecules, causing the intermolecular bonds to break (1). The temperature of the material does not increase until the solid has changed state (phase) (1). Energy is then transferred to the kinetic energy store of the material.

3 The expanded polystyrene is less dense than water (1) or the mass of the water that the expanded polystyrene displaces is less than its own mass (1).

4 The blocks must all be at the same temperature (room temperature) as they have been in the room long enough for equilibrium to be reached (1). The students' hands are warmer. Aluminium is a good conductor of heat (1) so when the students touch it, the temperature difference leads to heat being conducted from their hands and the block feeling cold (1). The wooden block is an insulator that will not conduct heat from the students' hands so it feels warmer (1).

Extended responses
Worked example
1 *A model response would be:*

The flame transfers energy by conduction (1) to the atoms in the rods which causes the atoms in them to vibrate more (1). The copper, being a metal, has free electrons but the glass doesn't (1). The kinetic energy store of these free electrons is increased so they move more quickly (1) as they travel through the metal. The electrons collide with the ions in the metal, transferring energy to them from their kinetic store (1). In the glass, each atom can transfer energy only to neighbouring atoms: there are no free electrons to speed up the transfer (1).

Be the examiner

2 *The student would be awarded 2/6. There was no mention of conduction, convection, evaporation or radiation. The student did not mention the vacuum.*

A model response would be:

The plastic stopper is a poor conductor so prevents convection currents (1) being set up in the surrounding air. It also stops any evaporation of the liquid (1). Glass is also a poor conductor preventing energy transfer by conduction (1). The vacuum between the two layers of glass prevents energy transfer by both conduction and convection (1). The silvered surface reflects infrared radiation (it is also a poor emitter of infrared) (1) preventing energy loss by radiation (1).

Practice question

3 There is lots of space between particles of a gas so it is easy to compress (1).

When a gas is compressed, the volume of the gas decreases (1). This means there is less space for the particles so they will collide with each other and the walls of the container more often (1). Colliding with each other will increase their store of kinetic energy (1). This increased vibrational energy is a thermal store which means there is a temperature rise (1). The increased number of collisions with the container wall means there is an increased force applied to it. As force over area is pressure, the pressure increases (1).

Practical Physics

Practice questions

1–1 To determine the power using current × p.d. (1).

1–2 The heater will become very hot: take care to only hold it by the end with the wires and allow it to cool down (1).

1–3 To insulate the block to avoid heat loss (1) to the air by convection (1) so all the heat supplied to the block is used to heat it.

1–4 Power supplied, $P = I\,V = 36$ W (1). Energy supplied, $E = P\,t = 36 \times (14 \times 60) = \underline{30\,240\,J}$ (1).

Or energy supplied = V I t = $\underline{30\,240\,J}$ (2)

Change in temperature = $40 - 22 = 18\ °C$ (1)

Using $E = m\,c\,\Delta\theta$, rearranged to $c = \dfrac{E}{m\,\Delta\theta} = \dfrac{30\,240}{1.5 \times 18}$

= $\underline{1120}$ (1) J/kg°C (1)

1–5 $1120 - 900 = \underline{220\,J}$ difference (1). This result is not accurate. It is 20% out (1).

The calculated value is higher than the true value, suggesting more energy must have been supplied than was needed to heat the block (1). Some energy would have been transferred to the surroundings as heat (1).

2–1 The independent variable is the attribute of the experiment that is varied by the experimenter to cause changes to the dependent variable (1). In this case, it is the energy supplied (1).

2–2 The dependent variable is the quantity being measured by the experimenter which varies due to changes made to the independent variable (1). In this case, the dependent variable is the mass of water collected (1).

2–3 $153 - 16 = \underline{137\,g}$ (or 0.137 kg) (1)

2–4 Power supplied, $P = I\,V = 6.4 \times 12 = 76.8$ W (1). Energy supplied, $E = P\,t = 76.8 \times (60 \times 10) = 46\,080\,J$ (1).

Or energy supplied = V I t = $\underline{46\,080\,J}$ (2)

Use $L_F = \dfrac{E}{m} = \dfrac{46\,080}{0.137} = \underline{340\,000}$ (1) J/kg (1)

Mathematics

Be the examiner

2 Answer C is correct. The temperature loss, $\Delta\theta$, is correct (1). The energy has been calculated correctly (1) and used with the power (the rate of energy transfer) to find the time (1).

Answer A is incorrect as the final temperature has been used instead of the temperature difference.

Answer B is incorrect because 500 has been used as the mass not 0.5 kg. Zeros are also missing from the (wrong) answer.

Practice questions

3 $\rho = \dfrac{m}{V} = \dfrac{0.004}{2.072 \times 10^{-7}} = \underline{19\,310\ kg/m^3}$ (1)

4 $L_F = \dfrac{E}{m} \Rightarrow E = L_F \times m = 3.4 \times 10^5 \times 20 = \underline{6\,800\,000\,J}$ (1)

5 4.4 ml $= 4.4 \times 10^{-6}$ m^3

$\rho = \dfrac{m}{V} = \dfrac{0.05}{4.4 \times 10^{-6}} = \underline{11\,363\ kg/m^3}$ which rounds to 11 400 kg/m^3 (1). The figure is lead (1).

6 For a gas, pressure × volume = a constant.
$P_1 \times V_1 = P_2 \times V_2$ (1)

$V_2 = \dfrac{P_1 \times V_1}{P_2} = \dfrac{1.2 \times 10^5 \times 8}{1.6 \times 10^5} = \underline{6\ cm^3}$ (1)

7 $L_V = \dfrac{E}{m} \Rightarrow m = \dfrac{E}{L_V} = \dfrac{360\,000}{2.3 \times 10^6} = \underline{0.16\ kg}$ (1)

8 Using $P = \dfrac{F}{A}$ the pressure of the elephant on the floor =

$\dfrac{1020 \times 9.8}{0.5} = \underline{19\,992\ Pa}$ (20 kPa) (1)

The pressure of the presenter on the floor = $\dfrac{50 \times 9.8}{0.0074}$
= $\underline{66\,216\ Pa}$ (660 kPa) (1).

The presenter will damage the floor (1) because a pressure of 660 kPa is greater (accept >) than 200 kPa (1). (Accept the elephant won't damage the floor (1) because 20 kPa is smaller than (or <) 200 kPa (1).)

10 Waves

Overview

Practice questions

1

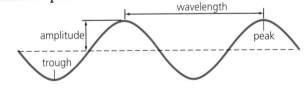

Peak and trough (1); amplitude (1); wavelength (1).

2 Only P-waves can be detected on the opposite side of the Earth (1) as only they can travel through the liquid outer core. S-waves can only travel through solids (1).

3 The waveform contains 4.5 waves so each wave lasted

$30 \div 4.5 = 6.67$ s (1) $f = \dfrac{1}{T} = \dfrac{1}{6.67} = 0.15$ Hz (1)

Extended responses

Worked example

1. *A model response would be:*

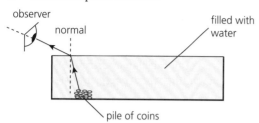

1 mark for correct rays; 1 for correct arrow direction.

The coins reflect light rays, in all directions. A light ray that reflects to hit the boundary of the water and air will change direction (1) because of the change in density. The light travels from a more dense material (water) to a less dense one (air) (1). This results in the light ray being directed away from the normal (1) (a line perpendicular to the water surface). This ray is now directed towards the eye, so the coins can be seen (1).

Be the examiner

2. *The student would be awarded 3/6. Refraction incorrectly named as reflection losing a mark. The frequency does not change but the wavelength does, although whether it is bigger or smaller isn't specified. The wave speed does decrease, so that is correct. The change of depth was not mentioned. The diagram scored 1 mark for the parallel lines. Overall this answer has correct ideas mixed in with incorrect ones.*

   A model response would be:

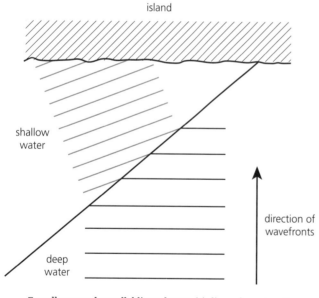

Equally spaced parallel lines drawn (1); lines closer together than in deep water (1).

As the waves hit the boundary between the deep and shallow water, refraction occurs (1). The change in depth changes the speed of the waves, slowing them down (1) which causes a change in direction (1). The wavelength decreases but the frequency remains the same (1). The energy of the wave remains the same which is why so much destruction was caused.

Practice question

3. X-rays are high-frequency, short-wavelength rays that can penetrate most materials so a bomb or gun can be easily seen (1). They are highly ionising (1) so should not be routinely used on people. Operators of the machines must take precautions to limit exposure (1). Microwaves are longer wavelength, lower frequency rays (1) with less penetrating ability but they can be used to create images through clothes (1). They are not ionising (1) but at high intensities can heat water molecules in the body.

Practical Physics

Practice questions

1–1 The frequency increases (1).

1–2 Count how many waves pass a point (1) in one second (1).

Or count how many waves pass a point in a certain time and divide the answer by that time (1) to get how many pass in one second (1).

1–3 A strobe light will flash on and off (1). If the flashing of the strobe is altered to exactly match the frequency of the waves (1), the waves will appear to stand still (1) and the wavelength can be measured more easily.

1–4 Using $v = \dfrac{s}{t} = \dfrac{0.3}{1.5} = 0.2$ m/s (1)

To find the frequency: $960 \div 120 = 8$ Hz (1)

Rearrange $v = f\lambda$ to give $\lambda = \dfrac{v}{f} = \dfrac{0.2}{8} = \underline{0.025 \text{ m}}$ or $\underline{2.5 \text{ cm}}$ (1)

2–1 A transverse wave (1)

2–2 A metre rule / long ruler / tape measure (1)

2–3 1.5 waves (1) $\lambda = \underline{0.67 \text{ m}}$ or $\underline{67 \text{ cm}}$ (1)

2–4 Amplitude $= 4.4 \div 2 = \underline{2.2 \text{ cm}}$ (or $\underline{0.022 \text{ m}}$) (1)

2–5 $f = \dfrac{1}{T} = \dfrac{1}{0.02} = 50$ Hz (1)

$v = f\lambda = 50 \times 0.67 = \underline{33.5 \text{ m/s}}$ (1)

2–6 Too small a mass would not keep the string taut so it would simply wobble and no standing wave would be seen (1). Too large a mass would make the string too tight so the amplitude of the wave would be too small to see (1).

2–7 The wooden bridge is where one node is formed (1), the other being at the vibration generator, *or* it provides the point for the wave to reflect from (1) *or* it allows you to easily change the length of the string (1).

Mathematics

Be the examiner

2. Answer C is correct.

Using $v = f\lambda$ rearranged to $f = \dfrac{v}{\lambda} = \dfrac{25}{10} = \underline{2.5 \text{ Hz}}$ (1)

To find the time, rearrange $v = \dfrac{s}{t}$ to $t = \dfrac{s}{v} = \dfrac{6000}{25} = 240$ s $= \underline{4 \text{ minutes}}$ (1).

Answer A is incorrect because the formula $v = f\lambda$ has been incorrectly rearranged to give $f = v\lambda$

In the second part, $v = \dfrac{s}{t}$ has not been rearranged to $t = \dfrac{s}{v}$

Answer B is incorrect because the units of frequency are Hz, not m/s.

In the second part 6 km has not been converted into 6000 m.

Practice questions

3. $\lambda = \dfrac{v}{f} = \dfrac{350}{70} = \underline{5 \text{ m}}$ (1)

4. $A = 34 \text{ m} \div 2 = 17 \text{ m}$ (1) $\lambda = \dfrac{v}{f} = \dfrac{23}{0.067} = \underline{340 \text{ m}}$ (1)

5   $f = \dfrac{v}{\lambda} = \dfrac{3 \times 10^8}{700 \times 10^{-9}} = \underline{4.3 \times 10^{14}}$ Hz (1)

6   $\lambda = \dfrac{v}{f} = \dfrac{3 \times 10^8}{6 \times 10^{14}} = 5 \times 10^7$ m = $\underline{500 \text{ nm}}$ (1). This means

the light is green (1).

7   For the P waves $t = \dfrac{s}{v} = \dfrac{700}{10} = 70$ s and for the S waves

$t = \dfrac{700}{4} = 175$ s.

The difference is 175 – 70 = $\underline{105 \text{ s}}$ or $\underline{1 \text{ minute } 45 \text{ s}}$ (1).

8   $343 \div 2.28 \times 10^{-2} = \underline{15\,000 \text{ Hz}}$ (1)

9   Knowing that microwaves travel at the speed of light, 3×10^8:

$3 \times 10^8 \div 6 \times 10^{10} = \underline{0.005 \text{ m}}$ or $\underline{0.5 \text{ cm}}$ (1)

10   $107 \div 82.41 = 1.30$ m (the wavelength). The string holds half a wavelength so is $1.30 \div 2 = \underline{0.65 \text{ m}}$ long (1).

11 Electromagnetism

Overview

Practice questions

1

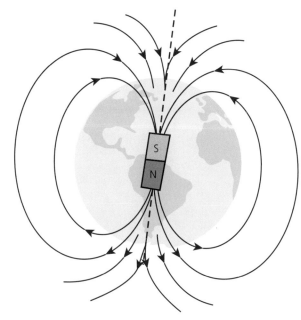

Correct pattern of lines (1), arrow direction (1), N and S correct (1).

The north pole of a bar magnet will be attracted to the south pole of another magnet so the Earth's magnetic poles are the opposite of what we normally call them.

2   The force acts without the magnets touching (1). The magnets repel or push apart (1).

3   Copper, Gold and Carbon ticked (1)

4

 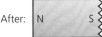

(1)

They are attracted together (stick or join together) (1).

5   Thumb: force (or movement), First finger: (magnetic) field, Second finger: (electric) current (1).

6–1   The wire will now spin clockwise (1).

The wire will return to spinning anti-clockwise (1).

6–2   Larger (greater or increased) potential difference (or voltage) and stronger magnet (1).

Do not accept more coils/more wire.

Extended responses

Worked example

1   *A model response would be:*

Closing the switch causes a current to flow through the wire. Iron filings sprinkled on the card (1) will make a pattern of concentric circular rings (1), more defined nearer the wire, less defined further away. The iron filings become induced magnets which line up along the magnetic field (1) that is generated by the electric current and at right angles to it (1). Moving a plotting compass (a small compass) around the circles on the card will show the direction of the field (1) (or using the right-hand grip rule: the current direction is down through the card so pointing the thumb of the right hand down, the curl of the fingers will give the direction of the field). In this case it is clockwise (1).

Be the examiner

2   *The student would be awarded 2/6. 'Magnetic charge' is incorrect, losing a point. The contacts are pushed together, they are not attracted to each other. The starter motor circuit becomes complete or closed, it is not a 'short circuit'. It is correct to say the starter motor circuit starts the engine but further details on how a petrol engine works are not required.*

A model response would be:

Turning the key completes a circuit to supply current to the electromagnet (1). This causes the electromagnet to generate a magnetic field (1) which attracts the shorter part of the iron arm towards the electromagnet (1). The iron arm pivots, pushing the contacts together (1) to complete the starter motor circuit (1). The starter motor starts the engine (1).

Practice question

3   The current flows through the coil, producing a magnetic field at right angles to it (1). This field is repelled by the field of the large magnet so the wire experiences a force at right angles to the direction of the current and the direction of the magnetic field (1). The other side of the wire experiences an equal and opposite force so, because the wire is on a pivot, the coil turns (1). The ends of the coil are attached to the two parts of the split-ring commutator. The ring touches the carbon brushes allowing the circuit to be complete but also allowing the coil to continue to spin (1). The circuit is momentarily broken when the coil is vertical but it has inertia that allows it to continue to turn until the opposite brush can make a connection with the split ring. When this happens, the current around the coil reverses so the forces are in the same direction as before (1). The direction of the spin is given by applying Fleming's left-hand rule to each side of the coil. In this case, the paired forces cause the coil to spin clockwise (1).

Practical Physics

Practice questions

1–1   Use the insulated wire (1) to wrap as many coils as possible around the iron rod (1) packing the coils as close together as possible (1). When a current flows through the insulated wire, it will induce a magnetic field with strong field lines at right angles to the current, so connect the wire to the power supply and set it to 12V (the largest voltage possible) (1). If bare copper wire were used, it would effectively become a single coil and allow current to be conducted through the iron rod (1). The iron rod should be chosen because the steel rod would become a permanent magnet that can't be switched off (1).

1–2 The wire (and the iron rod) will get hot (1) because there is little (or no) resistance in the circuit (it is a short circuit) so the current will be very high (1).

1–3 The power supply has detected a current above its set threshold (or the current is too high) (1). (Accept the power supply has a thermal cut-out or the power supply got too hot.) Reset the power supply (or reset the trip switch), or allow the power supply to cool down for a while (1).

Mathematics

Be the examiner

2   Answer B is correct:

To find the current: $I = V \div R = 12 \div 2 = 6$ A (1)

Rearrange $F = BIL$ to $B = \dfrac{F}{IL}$

$B = 0.6 \div (6 \times 0.1) = \underline{1\,T}$ (1)

Answer A is incorrect because the current was calculated with $I = V \times R$ instead of $I = V \div R$.

Answer C is incorrect because the formula has not been entered into the calculator properly. The 0.1 needs to be

part of the divisor as in answer B, i.e. $B = 0.6 \div \left(\dfrac{12}{2} \times 0.1\right)$.

Practice questions

3    $F = mg = 0.005 \times 9.8 = 0.049$ N (1)

$B = \dfrac{F}{IL} = 0.049 \div (3.5 \times 0.05) = \underline{0.28\,T}$ (1)

4    $L = 0.04 \times 300 = 12$ m (1)

$F = BIL = 0.3 \times 1.2 \times 12 = \underline{4.3\,N}$ (1)

5   Each additional 10 coils picks up 3 paperclips so $4 \times 3 = \underline{12\ paperclips}$ (1)

6–1 Using the left-hand-rule: to the left (1)

6–2 $0.4 \times 20 \times 0.05 = 0.4$ N (1)

6–3 Using $V/I = R$: $12 \div 20 = 0.6\ \Omega$ (1)

Using $V/R = I$: $24 \div 0.6 = 40$ A (1)

6–4 $0.4 \times 40 \times 0.02 = \underline{0.32\ N\ a\ lower\ force}$ (1)